DEBRETT'S

A–Z of
Modern Manners

Debrett's A–Z of Modern Manners
Published by Debrett's Limited
16 Charles Street
Mayfair
London W1J 5DS

SPECIAL ARTICLES: Susannah Jowitt
CONTRIBUTING AUTHOR: Elizabeth Wyse
ADDITIONAL TEXT: Jo Bryant, Sarah Corney, Ruth Massey

SENIOR MANAGING EDITOR: Jo Bryant
HEAD OF PUBLISHING: Elizabeth Wyse

DESIGN AND TYPESETTING: Smith & Gilmour, London
ILLUSTRATIONS: John Spencer
COVER DESIGN: Smith & Gilmour, London

ISBN 978-1-870520-75-1

Printed and bound by Graphicom – Vicenza, Italy
Visit us at www.debretts.com

FSC
Mixed Sources
Product group from well-managed
forests, and other controlled sources
www.fsc.org Cert no. CQ-COC-000015
© 1996 Forest Stewardship Council

DEBRETT'S

A–Z of
Modern Manners

'What do you think of modern civilisation?'

'I think it would be a good idea.'

MAHATMA GANDHI

AEROPLANES to AWAKE, STAYING

AEROPLANES

In cramped conditions, 35,000 feet above sea level, good manners are paramount. Do not intrude on to your fellow passengers' territory: keep elbows firmly tucked in; ease your chair gently into a reclining position, which will avoid a sudden invasion of the limited legroom of the passenger behind. If you have children, ensure that they do not kick, jolt, or otherwise interfere with, the seat in front. Drink in moderation; boisterous behaviour will irritate your fellow passengers. Friendly conversation with your neighbours can be enjoyable, but choose your topics. Many people are terrified of flying, and will not take kindly to jokes about turbulence, hijackers or the competence of the flight crew; such talk may even get you arrested.

Stay relaxed when embarking or disembarking. Help the elderly (or those of diminutive stature) to stow (or remove) luggage in the overhead lockers. Behave courteously towards the flight crew and thank them for their service during the flight. Never use the words 'trolley-dolly' or try to chat them up. They've heard it all before. Do not barge your way to the exit as the plane doors open — even the sharpest elbows will not ensure that you reach the terminal any faster.

AFFECTION, PUBLIC DISPLAYS OF

Being overly affectionate in public is embarrassing for those who are forced to witness private moments. Holding hands, being close and quick kisses are acceptable, but excessive physical intimacies should be reserved for the bedroom.

AFTERSHAVE

Aftershave should never be overpowering. People don't want to be able to smell you before they see you.

AGE

Children are proud to be getting older. It's the rest of us, especially those who feel they are rapidly approaching their second childhood, who have a problem with revealing our age. Could this be because we live in a society that is obsessed with the cosmetic appearance of ageing, that despises old people rather than venerates their experience, that no longer prizes old things but discards them as obsolescent, whether they are microwaves or celebrities?

We can hug to ourselves the maxims that 'Age is but a state of mind' and, 'You're only as old as the person you feel', but only the most confident can truly cope with the inevitable judgement that is associated with any mismatch between your looks and your actual age. It is cold comfort to remind yourself that anyone who asks you to reveal your age is just plain rude. If you are asked to guess, then head into the land of flattery rather than more perilous uncharted territories, and add or subtract generously, according to which age the other craves. For boors who insist on questioning you about your age, laugh it off with an obvious exaggeration.

The trouble is, in our Big Brother world, officialdom is constantly poised to box you into an age bracket – and they won't be fobbed off with cuteness. Next time you are requested to reveal your age, ask the doctor, bureaucrat

or nosy parker to consider the following answer:
your chronological age is a matter of years in existence,
your physical age is more than just counting the wrinkles,
your psychological age is growing, and your emotional
age is maturing. Above all, forget the encroaching physical
manifestations of age – plastic surgery is only a temporary
dam against the flood – and concentrate every fibre of
your being on not being mentally old.

ALLERGIES

In these days of heightened food awareness, allergies can
be a major headache for the host or hostess. Allergies can
range from the life-threatening to the merely discomforting.
Food aversions, on the other hand, are psychological;
people can convince themselves that hated foods cause
an allergic reaction, with no actual basis for this belief.

Obviously anyone who has a severe allergy must inform
their host, clearly and succinctly, about the nature of their
problem. The host must take this information seriously
and ensure that everything has been done to avert a disaster.
In certain circumstances (a large catered wedding breakfast,
for example), offering to bring your own packed lunch or
supper might be helpful.

A more circumspect approach should be taken for
those with less serious allergies. The potential seriousness
of the problem should be weighed up against the offence
and inconvenience that it will cause to the host. Presenting
someone with a long, and varied, list of foods to which

you have a mild aversion is quite unacceptable; on the other hand, if one – commonly served – food will make you feel ill and uncomfortable, the host should be told. Whatever the seriousness of the problem, once the host has been informed, they should ensure that the offending food is withdrawn. Teasing, cajoling or hectoring someone about a 'supposed' food intolerance is simply bad manners.

ANGER

'Anger fed is dead – 'Tis starving makes it fat.'
EMILY DICKINSON

In a world where cool self-possession is the Holy Grail of behaviour, anger would seem to be at the unacceptable end of the spectrum; yet anger can clear the air instantaneously, making us feel intensely alive. Sulking – the younger brother of anger – does none of this and can lead to real festering and real trouble.

But blowing your top can have fall-out, so be prepared to pay the price for words shot out in anger. Never forget that the joy of fury is one-sided: you may thrill to the rush of blood to the head, the excitement of finally being brave enough to say what you want; but the other person may just see a bug-eyed lunatic spitting out insults. So enjoy anger, but use it sparingly. Use it wisely – it can rebound on its perpetrator. Employ devastating logic rather than insults, even when your ire is at its peak. Finally, if the tables are turned and the anger is directed at you, just laugh – there is no better way of deflating someone else's balloon of hot air.

APERITIFS

An aperitif is a pre-lunch or dinner drink that stimulates the appetite and prepares the palate for food. Traditional choices include chilled dry sherry (sipped from a small stemmed glass), vermouth (fortified white wine served over ice in a tall glass) and Campari (served on the rocks or with orange). Spirit based drinks are also suitable; a cocktail, gin and tonic or a vodka and mixer. A simpler, and popular, option is a glass of chilled white wine or champagne.

When offered an aperitif as a guest, check what other people are drinking or ask what's on offer before requesting something your host may not have. *See also Digestifs*

APOLOGISING

A sincere apology should always be offered when your actions have had a negative impact on other people. Even if you do not fully understand why someone is so upset, respect their feelings, and accept that your actions are the root of the problem. Don't pass the buck, or use your apology as a way of blaming someone else. Take full responsibility for your actions. On the other hand, resist the (very English) urge to apologise for other people's actions. If someone barges into you, a muttered "Sorry" is misplaced. Constant, needless apologising devalues the currency, and will lessen the impact of a genuine, heartfelt *mea culpa*.

An apology will be much more persuasive if you acknowledge the fault: "I'm sorry I was so late" is more specific than a simple "I'm sorry", and actually recognises the other person's grievance. Never temper your apology with accusations or insinuations: it will negate its impact. If you have committed a real *faux pas* consider sending a handwritten note — but only after you have offered a verbal apology, otherwise it will look like cowardice.

If you are offered a genuine apology, acknowledge it graciously and accept it. The urge to elicit grovelling self-abasement is both childish and offensive.

APPLAUSE

Hand-clapping is the usual way of demonstrating approval or recognising achievement. Cheering and whooping should be kept to a minimum and whistling avoided. A slow handclap signals discontent from an audience that has been kept waiting. Booing a performer is never acceptable.

At the opera, applaud after the overture (before curtain-up), after an impressive aria (but never while someone is singing), at the end of a scene or act and, of course, at the end of the production. It is also the norm to clap the conductor when they take to the podium before the performance, after the interval and at the end (when the orchestra also takes a bow). At seated musical concerts, applaud between different compositions, but do not clap between movements within a piece. At the theatre, applause is expected at the end of each act, after a notable scene or moment ('a handbag?!') and at the end of a production.

At formal dinners or wedding receptions, the speakers are applauded before and after their speech. At award

dinners, prize-givings or similar ceremonies, a brief spell of applause is expected after the name of a winner or group of winners is announced. Further applause is expected after the acceptance speech.

APPLES

At the dinner table, apples should be cut into quarters and the core removed from each piece. You can then use your fingers to eat the quarters. Elsewhere, just hold and crunch.

ARGUMENTS

'Arguments are to be avoided: they are always vulgar and often convincing.'
OSCAR WILDE

Oscar Wilde, a man who honed the art of disagreeing politely into a dangerous conversational weapon, joked that a world without arguments or dissension would be grey indeed, and often the most colourful of arguments are those that do not descend into anger, remaining untainted by the red mist of rage. After all, the 'aim' of an argument should not be solely to win, but to progress the basic understanding of the issue at hand – and this is achieved more easily if everyone remains calm.

One rule of thumb is always to be *more* civil than the person you are arguing with; this will ensure that you retain your grip on the moral high ground. Shouting loudly to make your point is excusable in primary school but compromises your adult dignity. Argue about facts, not the personalities of the people with whom you're arguing. Avoid '-isms' at all costs; the use of labels leaves you wide open to accusations of generalisation and makes people instantly defensive. Work towards agreement, not point-scoring. Concede a point when you have no response to it. If you are arguing a point based on bias or intuition alone, have the honesty to admit it – this arms you with a reputation for being reasonable, which confers more power than just ranting. One effective tool is to apologise on the spot if you've said something you might regret later.

If all this sounds far too staid and dull, don't despair: an argument is never just a polite debate – it has a pinch more spice than that. The clenched teeth, the unbroken eye contact, the ebb and flow of ideas can be both electrifying and exciting. There is an intimacy in a good argument that has nothing to do with the issues being addressed, and that is precisely because a good argument is a team effort. Underlying all the disagreement is an agreement that the other person's opinion is valid, that you are at least going to listen to their side of the argument. For some people, the opposite of talking isn't listening, the opposite of talking is waiting for the other person to stop talking or – even worse – shouting over them. Do not argue with these people, it's just not worth the effort.

Finally, the Last Word. For some people, the Last Word is what an argument is all about; somehow he who speaks last, wins. Tempting as it may be to take this low road through an argument, try to resist. And that is our Last Word.

ARROGANCE

Arrogant people are blessed. They are lucky enough to be thick-skinned, brandishing their own certainty and lack of self-doubt or humility as they ride roughshod over the petty issues of other, lesser mortals. Their ability to remain unbowed, cantering through life without a care about the effects of their actions on those around them is enviable, but the effect of arrogance is distinctly undesirable.

Arrogant people are, quite simply, rude. People who have no self-doubt, who proceed without looking left and right to check the feelings of those around them are not people we should be rushing to befriend. Unfortunately, arrogance — that overbearing pride and superiority shown towards perceived inferiors — is now all too often associated with the drive to succeed, to get on, not to be held back by others. Do not be tempted by this empty formula: we train our children to be considerate of others, why do we imagine that a vital life-skill should ebb away in the name of a good business deal? Remember the American proverb, 'Arrogance is a kingdom without a crown.'

ART GALLERIES

Respect the rule of silence; don't stand in front of the paintings for a long time, or barge in front of other people. Wear any specialist knowledge lightly, and don't lecture companion(s). It's not necessary to like or understand everything, but keep strong opinions to yourself ("Call that art!" or "My two-year old does better!").

ARTICHOKES, GLOBE

The leaves of an artichoke should be peeled off one by one, starting with the outer leaves. Hold each leaf by its pointy tip and dip the base in the butter or sauce. Eat just the tender, rounded base of each leaf, and leave the rest. Place discarded leaves on the side of the plate. When you reach the centre, the smaller leaves and hairy choke can be cut away to reveal the heart. This is cut into pieces and eaten with a knife and fork. Finger bowls and napkins are a useful accompaniment.

ASPARAGUS

Hot asparagus is usually served with melted butter or hollandaise; cold asparagus with vinaigrette. Asparagus is best eaten in season, from the beginning of May to mid-June.

Unless asparagus is a vegetable accompaniment to a dish, or covered in sauce, it should be eaten with the fingers. The asparagus spear should be picked up towards the end of the stem, dipped in any accompanying sauce and lowered into the mouth, bite by bite. There's no need to chew through the tough, woody ends of the stems; they should be left neatly on the side of the plate.

AWAKE, STAYING

'Sleeping is no mean art: for its sake one must stay awake all day.'
FRIEDRICH NIETZSCHE

We've all been there. Those expensive, elusive theatre tickets for the must-see show ... and in the warm, dark intimacy of the theatre, you've fallen asleep before the end of the first act. Then there's the head-nodding on the train, the snoring during the spa treatment, the dinner party where you feel your eyes rolling inexorably up into your head, even as you see the horrified expression of the person who's still in the middle of a conversation with you. We live fast-paced, frenetic lives, and when we nod off during the day, it's just our systems trying to catch up. Yet it is possible to adjust patterns of behaviour, step off the hamster wheel, and take control of our sleeping patterns.

An hour of sleep before midnight is worth two after: so going to bed earlier and getting up earlier instantly makes you feel more rested and lively. The trouble is, this is unfashionable and potentially antisocial, so it's hard to implement. Avoid the jolt-crash cycle of caffeine and 'energy-boosting' sugary snacks, and choose instead herbal teas and slow-release foods like oatcakes or bananas.

Alternatively, you can just give up the unequal struggle and become comfortable with your cat-napping: warn people to pinch you in theatres, ask someone to wake you before your stop on train journeys. If you do commit the sin of falling asleep in a social context then apologise profusely, explain why you are exhausted (insomnia, jet lag, overwork), make your excuses and leave immediately. No one, not even a bore, should have to converse with a narcoleptic.

See also Zzzzz

BABIES TO **BUSINESS TRIPS**

BABIES

A baby is below the age where manners can reasonably be asked of it, so we reserve our judgement for the parents. Unfortunately, for some parents the biological act of procreation is a signal for normal standards of behaviour to be abandoned. As a new parent, it is your duty to rein in your boundless enthusiasm for this bundle of joy. Tolerance works both ways, but it is simply unrealistic to expect the rest of society to be as happy and proud as you.

Baby photos are only interesting for under one minute. Never show off video footage to anyone but members of the tightest family circle. The precise timing of tooth-cutting, first word, first solid food and first steps are details that only you and your health professional actively need to know. Do not imagine that it is suddenly tolerable to boast about the consistency of stools, that it's somehow admirable to lose the power of speech as you gurgle at the child or that it's acceptable to react to the blood-curdling yells of a baby, with an insouciant shrug and the words, "Don't worry, he's just a bit tired". This blindness is not acceptable behaviour from an adult.

Polite people should have the good manners to admire the baby; they should not tut-tut at the first whimper from a child, and should appreciate that over-tired parents are dangerously frazzled. Ultimately, however, it is the parents' responsibility to contain and control any baby-related mayhem. Parents say to each other of babies, "One's a pet, two's a zoo," as an exculpatory panacea for whatever chaos is being unleashed. We say, look to the zoo-keeper.

BAD NEWS

Being the bearer of bad news is an unenviable job – and one where the gravity of the task often drives rationality out of the window. Whether the news is of bereavement or redundancy, common sense dictates that you aim for some sort of physical closeness with the receiver of bad news; establish eye-contact on the same level and – if you know them well – a physical gesture, such as putting an arm around their shoulder, may be appropriate. You should speak slowly and clearly, leaving no room for uncertainty (which could lead to misleading hope) and pre-empting as many of their questions as possible, so that they don't have to pull themselves together to speak. Choose the place in which you deliver the news sensibly – make sure you will be uninterrupted, that your mobile is switched off and that you can give the receiver your undivided attention.

Hold yourself back from babbling out words of empty comfort or, even worse, trying to fill the silence with jokey 'silver-lining' comments – "At least you won't have to put up with the canteen's sandwiches anymore!" The role of the bad-news-giver is to make the communication as pain-free as possible, but not to mitigate the bad news itself.

At the more devastating end of the bad news spectrum, just make sure they know that you're going to be there for them as long as they want you – no glancing at your watch, or checking your text messages – and into the weeks and months beyond. Time is a great healer, but it has a long waiting list; the knowledge that you don't have to be alone while you're on it is of undeniable comfort to the grieving.

BALDNESS

Accept it. What's left should be cut very short or shaved.
Never be tempted by a comb-over.

BANANA, EATING

If you're eating a banana at the dinner table, peel it fully,
and use a fork to cut off bite-sized pieces. In all other
situations, revert to primate manners — hold, peel and bite.

BAR MITZVAHS AND BAT MITZVAHS

Bar Mitzvahs and Bat Mitzvahs are Jewish coming-of-age
ceremonies, held when a boy turns 13 (a Bar Mitzvah) and
when a girl turns 12 (a Bat Mitzvah). They are the most
important rites of passage in the Jewish faith.

Formal invitations are sent out by the parents, inviting
guests to the ceremony at the synagogue, and to attend the
reception afterwards at their home/venue, which can range
from a festive meal to a lavish party. Guests should respond
with a handwritten reply. For less formal celebrations,
invitations are often a note or postcard, or by word of
mouth. Presents are given by guests but, as with a wedding,
are either sent in advance or taken to the post-ceremony
celebrations — never take the present along to the synagogue.

Guests should arrive at the synagogue on foot (devout
Jews do not drive during the day on Saturdays) and dress
appropriately. Men should wear a formal suit and skullcap,
women smart day dress (ensuring their arms are covered

above the elbow and their legs above the knee) and a hat.
Men and women will often be seated separately. While there
is usually singing during the ceremony, some of the service
may involve standing in silence. Appropriate times to
leave the room may be observed from the actions of the
congregation. Keep your mobile phone turned off –
many Jews do not use electrical devices on Saturdays.

BARBECUES

Ensure that the barbecue is lit and ready before guests arrive.
Panic-stricken recourse to paraffin can be discouraging,
especially when guests are hungry. Provide enough
comfortable seats for all the guests; juggling food and drink
while standing will diminish your guests' enjoyment. Make
sure there is plenty of shade; if you are fortunate enough
to have good weather, the sun may be hazardous. Provide
plentiful supplies of ice-cold water; it will keep your guests
hydrated, and may prolong the supply of chilled beer and
wine. Be aware of your neighbours; barbecues are highly
aromatic and, depending on wind direction and cooking
ability, neighbours may find themselves suffocated by acrid
black smoke or tantalising smells. Pre-empt the problem
altogether by inviting them.

Above all, don't make an exhibition of the cooking.
Comedy aprons, chef's hats and swaggering machismo as
the meat hits the grill are obtrusive and self-centred. Your
guests have come to eat and socialise, and should not feel
coerced into applauding a one-man show.

BARS

At a crowded bar respect the 'first come, first served' rule and wait your turn. Make eye contact with the bartender, and don't get frustrated if you are not served immediately. If unsure whether it's your turn, look around you and gesture 'after you' to anyone looking expectant.

Don't impose your rowdy drinking games or loud-spoken camaraderie on fellow-drinkers. If you accidentally jostle someone and spill their drink you should offer to replace it.

Always tip the staff in a bar with table service. This is generally ten per cent and may be added to the bill, but leave cash, or add it on to your final payment, if not. *See also Pubs*

BEACHES

The beach is an unusual public area where we strip down to the equivalent of our underwear. However, even in such *laissez-faire* surroundings, behaviour should be governed by consideration for others.

Respect other people's space and ensure that noise is at a minimum; keep at least a towel's width away from the next encampment. Shake towels out with full consideration of the wind direction. Music should only be played through headphones, never speakers. Team sports should be reserved for quiet, unpopulated stretches of sand. Respect the coastguard and take note of any signs or flags.

Swimwear should protect your modesty. Avoid thongs, micro-brief trunks and anything that goes transparent on contact with water. Try not to stare, or ogle, at fellow sun-

bathers – particularly if they are struggling to dress or undress discreetly. Sarongs and T-shirts should be worn in shops, bars and restaurants, so cover up when not on the beach. On departure, clear up all rubbish.

BEARDS

'How many cowards wear yet upon their chins the beards of Hercules and frowning Mars!'
WILLIAM SHAKESPEARE

Beards must be kept clean and in shape. Wash, shampoo and trim regularly. Watch out for froth (cappuccino, Guinness) and sauces (ketchup, mayonnaise). Comedy beards and goatees are to be avoided once you've left your student days behind you. *See also Stubble*

BELLBOYS

At smarter hotels or clubs bellboys open the door for you on arrival and departure and take your luggage to your room. It is usual to give them a tip (one or two pounds, dollars, etc., as appropriate, per item of luggage), which you should hand to them as they leave your room. *See also Hotels; Tipping*

BILL, PAYING THE

There is one abiding rule – the person who requests the pleasure, pays for the pleasure. So, as a simple point of etiquette, you should pick up the tab for a lunch, dinner or a raft of cocktails — whether dating or business-lunching — if you have invited the other person. But business lunches aside, life isn't simple, and dating even less so; all too often, the awkwardness that arrives at the table at the same time as the bill is less to do with etiquette than gender.

It is more likely than not that the man has been the one to invite his date out to dinner, so he should be the one to pay. But it's unfair if he has to pay every time — and some women are actively insulted if men always insist on paying. On the other hand, if he cocks his eyebrow towards his date in the international gesture for "Perhaps it's your turn this time?" he could all too easily be judged cheap and ungentlemanly.

Men should be prepared to pay every time, but equally ready to concede under the following conditions: if she is adamant she must pay her way; if it is his birthday or a special occasion on which she wants to make the gesture of paying for him; or, in the case of steady couples, if she is quietly seeking to break the trend of the man paying every time.

Do not be tempted by the compromise solution: splitting the bill. That is fine for bigger restaurant gatherings (though never, ever niggle — the momentary victory of only paying for your soup is spoiled by the longer lasting defeat of your social credibility), but the greatest spoiler to romance is going Dutch. Going Chinese, however, is a different ballgame: as in many Asian countries, there is a strong etiquette at play. It is culturally unacceptable to pay the bill if your host is Asian but you should be seen to offer with a vague and speedy wave of your wallet, after which everyone's face is saved. *See also Going Dutch; Restaurants*

BIRTH ANNOUNCEMENTS

All family members and close friends should be phoned
as soon as possible after the birth and told the good news.
This is traditionally the responsibility of the father.

- Birth announcement cards, if used, should be printed
  in a simple, elegant style and read:
  James and Mary Robinson are happy to announce the birth of their son
  Thomas Charles
- The baby's date of birth and weight are included and a pink
  or blue ribbon may be attached.
- A short birth announcement can also be placed in a local
  or national newspaper if desired, for example:
  Robinson — On 20th February to James and Mary a son, Thomas Charles
- If the parents are not married, their surnames should be
  included:
  Robinson — On 20th February to James Robinson and Mary Jones a son,
  Thomas Charles
- In the case of single parents:
  Jones — On 20th February to Mary a son, Thomas Charles

BITCH, BEING A

Talking about someone behind their back is not the nicest
behaviour, and it's certainly not very enjoyable when it
happens to you. But therein lies the secret of being a good
bitch — the one who never gets caught out, never gets
overheard or reported back, and never actually hurts
anyone's feelings. There are few things more riveting than
a discussion of others' foibles and flaws and few better ways

of strengthening a friendship than bitching. It takes you outside the zone of traditional politeness and lets your friend into your confidence and intimacy. Bitching can also be extremely funny and serves as a cathartic release; better sometimes that you positively let off steam about your boss/mother/spouse to a neutral peer than always plunge into the dangerous waters of outright confrontation.

Just set some ground rules – don't be a bitch to those younger than you, don't bitch if you have any suspicion that your words might get back to their target, and, if you are the victim, take the wind out of their sails by agreeing with them.

BLACK TIE

If required, black tie (sometimes referred to as 'dinner jacket' or in America as 'tuxedo'), will be specified on invitations. Traditional black tie consists of:

- Black wool dinner jacket. Single-breasted with no vents, silk peaked lapels (or a shawl collar) and covered buttons.
- Black trousers – slightly tapered – with a single row of braid down each outside leg.
- White marcella evening shirt with a soft turn-down collar, worn with cufflinks and studs.
- Black bow tie must be hand tied; avoid novelty ties or colours.
- Highly polished or patent black lace-up shoes and black silk socks.
- A white silk scarf is an optional but traditional accessory. Cummerbunds or black evening waistcoats are rarely worn.

See also Bow Ties; Eveningwear; White Tie

BLACKBERRY™

The horror of the public BlackBerry™ can be mitigated by various points of etiquette – using an email filter, saying no to the Robocop look of cordless headset, avoiding the novelty ringtone at full volume, refraining from frequent glances at the device when in company.

When CrackBerry became the Webster Dictionary's word of the year in 2006, the hunched and silent phenomenon that is the 'Berry' addict became too mainstream to ignore. Worker bees and magnates argue that, in this day of 24/7, minute-by-minute developments, both dinner table *politesse* and a notch or two on the blood pressure monitor have to be sacrificed if their careers are at stake by not keeping up – wirelessly – when they're out of the office. Yet the sight of a corporate lunch party, all casting furtive glances at their little friend, lined up beside each plate like a modern-day napkin, is both laughable and rather sad.

Observing wireless etiquette will go some way towards mitigating the offence, but there's a simpler, more draconian conclusion. If you are a 'Berry' player then you clearly have no time off from work and you can't socialise – therefore you should not attempt to have a social life. Think of your friends. Their attempt to integrate you and your gadget is as if they are hanging around your desk, talking to you while you are trying to get your work done. This would be rude in an office environment – and it's equally rude in a social situation. So help your friends not to be rude – and just have a double date with your little electronic friend in the privacy of your own home or office.

BLIND DATES

'Let's face it: a date is a job-interview that lasts all night.'
JERRY SEINFELD

Blind dates are usually the result of the machinations of an eager matchmaker. They should be approached with caution and realism – the hit rate is often low because a third party is trying to direct cupid's arrow.

It is wise to gather some advance information. Utilise social networking sites, and quiz the matchmaker – this will provide useful background material and plenty of conversation for the date.

You must establish contact with your date beforehand to make arrangements – email is a convenient (and suitably anonymous) method of communication. Drinks are a more flexible option than dinner; the evening can be as short or as long as desired. You must also establish a way of recognising each other: for example, it could be decided that both of you will be carrying or reading a copy of the same newspaper.

If the match proves to be disastrous, excuses shouldn't be made too soon (you should stick around for two drinks) – spare a thought for the matchmaker, who will be waiting to hear about the progress of both parties with some anxiety. Send an email within a few days, letting the other party down gently. Don't berate the matchmaker for their bad judgement, or feel insulted by their recommendation.

If the evening works out well, exchange numbers, send a text message the following day (or within two days) and plan more dates. The matchmaker also deserves a bottle of something to say thank you. *See also Internet Dating; Matchmaking*

BLUFFING, SOCIAL

You're at a drinks party and someone hails you warmly by name and asks how you are. You have no idea who they are. Or someone asks what you think of the new leaks from the Cabinet. You only just stop yourself telling them not to worry, you've got a good carpenter and murmur instead that, oh yes, the rot started when spin doctors got ideas above their station. You are now a social bluffer.

Social bluffing is the attempt by people in a social gathering to balance their ignorance or bad memory with their overwhelming need to be polite or to appear better-informed than they actually are. If you can't remember someone's name, or don't know what someone is talking about and you just say so out loud, some might call it admirably direct. But the person opposite could feel hurt and offended that you don't think them memorable or rate their conversational sorties.

So we err on the side of the social bluffers, the people who go to any lengths to avoid such rudeness, resorting to the sorts of elaborate half-truths and gambits that would normally have us condemning their grasp of honesty. For the name-forgetter, the safest rule of thumb is to assume that no one remembers who you are – "Hello, I'm sure you don't remember me but I'm…," thereby prompting them to respond with their own name at the same time as charming them with your humility. Bluffing your way through your own ignorance is easier – simply repackage what they've just said as an interesting question, "So what do you think prompts such Cabinet leaks?".

BOASTING

The tendency to advertise your own skills, attributes or virtues is a childish trait, and the height of bad manners. While false modesty can also be irritating — a way of eliciting compliments from the unwilling listener — boasting is not an acceptable alternative. If you deserve praise, it will be forthcoming; nobody receives as many compliments as they would like; making up for the deficiency by complimenting yourself will only serve to make you thoroughly unpopular.

BODILY FUNCTIONS

We all have them, but they should never be brought up in conversation. *See also Illness, Discussing; Loo; Urinal; Wind*

BODY LANGUAGE

Body language is a series of silent signals that play a vitally important part in the impression you give to the world.

Negative signals include crossed arms, hunched shoulders and fiddling and fidgeting. Positive signals include good posture (naturally sitting up straight), appropriate eye contact (don't stare) and confident hand gestures (no pointing). During conversation, gently leaning towards the other person and nodding occasionally to acknowledge agreement conveys interest. A (genuine) smile is always a winner.

Good body language creates a positive air of confidence. It puts others at ease and, according to some research, makes you more sexually attractive. *See also Deportment*

BONES

It is usually not appropriate to pick up bones and gnaw on them. However, if you are at an informal gathering, such as a barbecue or picnic, it is fine to eat a chicken wing or spare rib with your fingers.

If you find a piece of bone in your mouth, manoeuvre it to the front from where it can be discreetly removed with thumb and forefinger and placed on the side of your plate. *See also Fish, Eating*

BOREDOM

The *ennui* that you experience when you are forced to listen to a boring conversation can be quite excruciating. But you must at all costs disguise, or dispense with, the physical manifestations of boredom – yawning, watering eyes, a fixed and glazed look, frequent glances at your watch, a tendency to cast your eyes around the room looking for an escape route. Instead, take the bull by the horns; interject, crack a joke, change the course of the conversation, introduce another person into the group, make a graceful exit.

If you have suffered from boredom yourself, you should be all too aware of the manifestations of boredom in others. Never risk being a bore by following these rules: listen to what people have to say; react to their conversation; ask questions; only hold forth if you are invited to; keep your obsessions to yourself; never lecture or harangue. Above all, be aware that a proper conversation requires the full participation of at least two people.

BORES, ESCAPING FROM

'Perhaps the world's second worst crime is boredom. The first is being a bore.'
CECIL BEATON

Talleyrand, on being buttonholed by a tedious fan in the Travellers Club, called over one of the servants and said, "Do you mind listening to the end of this man's story?" Some people have been known to pour wine over themselves in a desperate attempt to escape the panicky claustrophobia that is brought on by the bore at the office party, the wedding or the cocktail party. Others have had recourse to lies about mobile phone messages, prior engagements, stomach upsets and domestic emergencies.

The easiest, politest route is to listen silently – raptly, even – for a few minutes, then say, "How fascinating, but please, don't let me monopolise you," tap the next door person and introduce them before making a swift exit, stage right. At a wedding or cocktail party, it's fine to excuse yourself to get a drink or some food, or claim that the host/hostess needs helping – but this is harder in an office situation or in a pub.

If you are trapped by a bore, and you have lost all hope of escape, embrace the situation and try to out-bore the bore, while indulging in an enjoyable venting of spleen. With not a thought for politeness, wrench the conversational initiative away from him/her and start ranting about a subject close to your own heart. It's cathartic to get stuff off your chest and you may even scare off the bore who's unused to having the conversational baton stolen. *See also Travel Bores*

BORROWING

Borrowing is fraught with peril. Sometimes it is unavoidable and if you have friends much richer than you it is tempting to borrow. But once you have borrowed from a friend, you have unbalanced your relationship, tipped the scales from equal peers to that of bank manager and account holder. If you must borrow money from someone you know, then damage limitations might include setting up a standing order the very day of the loan. Even if it's for a tiny amount each month, the message is clear: that you fully intend to pay back your borrowing – unlike the 18th-century playwright Richard Sheridan who wrote, 'I handed one of my creditors an IOU and thought thank heavens that's settled.'

If you are a borrower of more frivolous items, the lines are a little more blurred. Borrowing a skirt, a book or a pair of earrings can be flattering; it implies that the person from whom you are liberating possessions has covetable taste. Just try not to stretch it, shrink it, lose it or spatter it with food. Above all, never fall into the trap of lending said item to the same friend years later with the words, "I never liked this, so you might as well have it". *See also Lending*

BOSSES

Good bosses listen to their staff. They recognise strengths, understand procedures (no matter how big or small) and set reasonable goalposts (that they don't shift). Praise, encouragement, and rewards are delivered promptly when due – and professional morale is gratifyingly high.

BOUNCERS

Bouncers should be treated with respect and not argued with; after all, it is in their power to throw you out of the club or refuse you entry if they take a dislike to you. Check the dress code of the club first to avoid disappointment on the night. If you do find you are not wearing the right attire for entrance accept this and leave the queue without causing a scene. Only the brave attempt bribery.

BOW TIES

'The finest clothing made is a person's skin, but, of course, society demands something more than this.'
MARK TWAIN

When an invitation states 'black tie', a gentleman is required to wear a dinner jacket and a bow tie. Bow ties should be black and hand-tied – avoid novelty or coloured ties.

How to tie a bow tie:
- Hang the tie around your neck, in place over the collar.
- Adjust the tie so that one end is slightly longer than the other, crossing the long end over the short.
- Bring the long end through the centre at the neck.
- Form an angled loop with the short end of the tie crossing left. Drop the long end at the neck over this horizontal loop.
- Form a similar angled loop with the loose long end of the tie and push this loop through the short loop.
- Tighten knot by adjusting the ends of both loops.
  See also Black Tie

BOWING

When being introduced to a member of the Royal Family
men should bow and women curtsey. The bow should be
made by bending from the neck or shoulders while briefly
lowering your eyes. Bow again when the member of the
Royal Family leaves. *See also Curtseying; Queen, HM The; Royal Family*

BREAD ROLLS

Bread rolls are eaten from a side plate to the left of a place
setting. You should break your roll into bite-sized pieces
that are eaten individually. Break off a new piece for each
mouthful, rather than dividing the roll into chunks in
advance. Butter, if desired, is taken from the butter dish
and placed on the edge of your side plate. Each piece, or
mouthful, is individually buttered. *See also Table Manners*

BREASTFEEDING

New mothers are encouraged to breastfeed for a minimum
of six months, but may find that attitudes to breastfeeding
in public, or in the workplace, are censorious and off-
putting. Negotiating this minefield requires sensitivity
and flexibility. While as a mother you may feel that you
have an absolute right to breastfeed wherever you choose,
you will probably find you have an easier time if you are
not aggressive about your rights, and remember that some
people (especially the older generation) are uncomfortable
about the whole issue. It is possible to breastfeed discreetly,

using specially adapted clothing, scarves or shawls to minimise self-exposure. It is also possible to choose locations that are a little out of the public eye.

If a mother has made an effort to breastfeed discreetly, she deserves to be treated with tact and sensitivity. Do not stare, or pass comment, or give her disapproving looks. She has made concessions to you; now you must reciprocate.

BREATH

Bad breath doesn't just put off prospective lovers, it puts off lovers of life, in fact, anyone but the undead. Breathing foulness on to people is the most obvious bar to sharing your life happily with other human beings. True oral *cognoscenti* know that bad breath can be averted by a simple routine of regular teeth-brushing, flossing and gargling with mouthwash. But how do you know if you have bad breath? If you are with family or a good friend, ask them. Immediately. If you are not, there is an easy test, much more reliable than the old cupping hand trick. Simply lick the inside of your wrist, wait a minute for it to dry, then smell.

It is impolite to have bad breath because it implies a lack of self-awareness and care for others' sensitivities, but it is far worse manners towards a close friend or family member not to somehow, subtly and kindly, tell them. So brace yourself and say firmly to them, "You would tell me if I had bad breath, wouldn't you? I have a sneaking suspicion that I might have terrible morning breath – can you check?" Only the densest individual wouldn't then ask you to do the same.

BUFFETS

At formal 'wedding-style' buffets, guests get called up table-by-table; you should go to get your food promptly when requested, as guests who are slow off the mark can hold up the conveyor belt. At parties with a buffet, timing is less crucial, but make sure you don't end up being the last one chewing. Food may be eaten standing up, so choose a fork-friendly selection that requires little or no cutting. Plates shouldn't be overloaded – it's better to go back for seconds than look like you haven't eaten for a week. *See also Parties*

BURPING

It may amuse you – and young children – but most people will find it offensive and unattractive.

BUSINESS CARDS

Exchanging business cards is common practice for business introductions and even some social ones. However, it is not seen as essential in this country and if you offer your card you should not necessarily expect one in return.

The standard business card is about the same size as a credit card. Your full name and usually your job title should be printed on it. Qualifications after your name may be added (leave off university degrees), but titles before the name are not usually included. Contact details such as phone numbers, fax number, email address and postal address should also appear.

BUSINESS TRIPS

Going on a business trip with colleagues can often seem
to re-draw the automatic lines of office etiquette; you're
suddenly in a situation where you're snoozing next to your
colleagues on the aeroplane, breakfasting with them,
sometimes even sunbathing with them around the pool
of the hotel. But don't be fooled by the enforced intimacy
of the trip into believing that work hierarchies aren't still
in place. You may have seen your boss in his swimming
trunks brandishing an umbrella-ed cocktail, but this
shouldn't alter your behaviour or respect towards him.

Avoid any hint of a compromising situation. Travel to
and from the trip separately from your colleagues if that is
possible. Other people always want to do things differently
from you – arrive at the airport hours earlier than you
would, or chat throughout the flight, for example – and
travelling separately will avoid awkwardness. Once there,
play the exercise card (especially swimming where it's hard to
be sociable while ploughing up and down the pool) to avoid
round-the-clock proximity to your workmates. Above all,
adopt a demeanour of benign tolerance for whatever bizarre
situation you find yourself in, be it a strip club in Frankfurt,
a bathhouse in Istanbul or a karaoke bar in Tokyo.

If you are on a solo business trip, don't be afraid to dine
alone in the hotel restaurant but always look purposeful,
absorbed and unselfconscious about your solitude. A book
is a crucial accessory. Don't be tempted to hide away and get
room service – do you really want to eat your supper and
sleep in the same room? *See also Office Politics*

CAMPING to CUTLERY

CAMPING

Show consideration for fellow campers. Don't encroach on neighbours' space. Keep your pitch tidy and take home any litter or deposit it in bins on site, recycling where possible. Use the lavatories provided and clean up after your pets.

Avoid loud conversation or music during antisocial hours. All outdoor lights should be turned off late at night when your neighbours may want to sleep. Do not start a campfire or barbecue too close to others' pitches.

Where a sea of tents stretches as far as the eye can see, such as at a music festival, note where you pitched your tent, and always carry a torch to avoid stumbling around the campsite after dark muttering "I'm sure it was here somewhere".

CANAPÉS

Negotiate a way through the canapé minefield by adopting a tactical approach. If you are hungry remember that it is very poor form to take two canapés at a time. Always try and eat a canapé in one mouthful, without overfilling your mouth or chewing vigorously mid-conversation. Watch your timing. Only tuck in when you aren't about to be introduced to someone. If a delicacy looks challenging or messy, politely decline and wait for something more manageable to appear.

Canapés are often served with complicated sticks, spoons or sauces. Check for discreetly placed dishes where apparatus can be discarded; never put something you've eaten off back on a tray that is still circulating. Equally, never double dip your canapé in the sauce. *See also Parties*

CANCELLING

In this time-starved age, one of the rudest things we can
do is to assume that someone else's time is not as precious
as platinum. If you cancel an engagement, remember that
you are wasting the other person's carefully apportioned
time; apologies are definitely in order.

The traditional rule of thumb for acceptable reasons
for cancellation was restricted to a death in the family or
a medical emergency. Nowadays, that has relaxed a little
but cancelling is all about timing. The clear-cut rules for
cancelling a hotel reservation can simply be applied for
all cancellations. If you pull out more than a month
beforehand, there is no penalty at all; between a month and
two days beforehand, there are varying but small amounts
of fallout; anything less than 48 hours and you start to incur
hefty charges; and if you cancel on the same day or, rudest
still, fail to show up altogether, then you have to pay the full
price. Hotel rooms may be expensive but friendships have
been known to founder on such cavalier behaviour.

Always apologise profusely, even if you're not actually
sorry you're cancelling. But keep it simple: if you've cancelled
early enough, the person doesn't necessarily need to know
why — a trivial reason can easily compound the offence.
Cancelling once (following the timing rules above) is perfectly
considerate; constantly postponing a meeting that you are
secretly dreading merely prolongs the agony and ends up
being rude and hurtful. Similarly, don't accept invitations
just to be polite and end up double-booking yourself: you'll
have to cancel one person in favour of the 'better offer',

thereby mortally offending the first if they ever find out. If you are the person who is being cancelled – the cancellee – look on the bright side of being blown out. Accept the cancellation gracefully, and don't punish the canceller with a peeved, hurt response. Above all, savour that unexpected night in with nothing to do. *See also Postponing*

CAR, GETTING INTO AND OUT OF

It is a courteous gesture for a man to open the car door for a woman, letting her get in first, before walking around and getting in himself. When getting out of cars, women should take care to swivel while keeping their knees together, especially when wearing a skirt.

CAREER

'Don't confuse having a career with having a life.'
HILLARY CLINTON

Manners maketh the future millionaire. Gone are the days when a snarling, pushy, take-no-prisoners, 'lunch is for wimps' executive was the role model. Those who build CVs from the age of five and demonstrate their skill at passing exams and gaining qualifications are now seen as single-minded geeks, hampered by a lack of proficiency in handling social and professional situations. Today, both employers and employees are acknowledging the importance of what are termed 'the softer skills'. Here the emphasis is on an easy grasp of manners, the confidence that comes from

knowing the appropriate response in any given situation and, above all, the ability to give the impression that you are thinking how your behaviour affects others. Such skills are initially vital at the interview stage (hence all the 'manners' courses now run by universities) and then crucial in both client situations and for harmonious office relations. Promotion favours the polite.

Ideally, those who have honed these skills and are successful in their careers should remember such manners outside the workplace, and realise that their own meteoric rise and current career importance might not be the most riveting thing for their friends and family. Successful careerists who've started to believe their own propaganda can easily turn into the most boring people in the room, especially to those who might not be in the conventional career mainstream: full-time parents, downsizers, or those who've just lost their own jobs. A successful career is gratifying news for your bank manager and boosts your self-esteem — but it is always rude to bang on about it.

CASINOS

'It can be argued that man's instinct to gamble is the only reason he is still not a monkey up in the trees.'
MARIO PUZO

The dress code in most casinos is smart casual; dress as though you are going to a smart restaurant. Top casinos are similar to private members' clubs. Guests are signed in by a member and there is often a dress code of jackets and ties.

If you have never gambled before, take some time to observe the different games. Stand near the tables but never sit; non-players will be asked to move. Novices should avoid tables where serious play is taking place. Bets should always be placed on the table, dealers are not allowed to take cash or chips directly from players. Never touch cards that are dealt face up; cards dealt face down should only be picked up with one hand. Take care of the cards – never bend them (some casinos view this as cheating) or put your drink on them.

If you run out of luck, lose graciously. Never swear, argue or, worse, accuse the dealer of cheating. Remember that they are always right. Equally, if you land a big win, you should tip the dealer. Gleeful shouting, victory dances, punching the air and gloating are all entirely inappropriate.

CAVIAR

Caviar – the roe of the sturgeon fish – is best eaten as simply as possible, served at room temperature, with a glass of vodka or champagne. Accompaniments such as sour cream, onions and lemon are popular, but a true connoisseur would never disguise the true taste of the caviar. The average portion is approximately 30 grams; it should be enjoyed in small quantities and not eaten in bulk.

Good caviar should not taste salty. Test it by placing a small amount on the fleshy part of your hand between your thumb and index finger; it should not smell. Once opened, caviar should be stored in a champagne flute in the fridge, never in the tin.

CHAMPAGNE

'A woman should never be seen eating and drinking, unless it be lobster salad and champagne, the only true feminine and becoming viands.'
LORD BYRON

Open the bottle gently without shaking to avoid spraying the champagne everywhere like a triumphant Formula One driver. Peel off the foil and remove the 'cage' that keeps the cork in place. Ease the cork off by keeping a light hold on it while twisting the bottle slowly – you're aiming for a gentle sigh, not a loud pop. Pour into proper champagne flutes, which can be filled up to the top. The tall narrow shape of the glass will preserve the bubbles. Hold it at the stem so your warm hands don't affect the temperature of the champagne. Champagne should be served chilled, so sit an opened bottle in an ice bucket in-between refills.

CHAT-UP LINES

"If I said you had a beautiful body, would you hold it against me?"

Male or female, young or not-so-young, chat-up lines are best avoided. Do you really want to be remembered for second-hand conversation? Remember the basics: eye-contact, confidence and a large dose of well-timed and appropriate humour. Keep them interested long enough to get a number (or something more ...). Ask them about themselves. Remember what they tell you. Make them laugh. Be interested and interesting. Never move things along too quickly or jump the gun: "Is it hot in here or is it you?"

CHEESE

Always use the cheese knife provided to cut cheese from a communal board, not your own butter knife. Round cheese must be treated like a cake: cut triangular portions. With a wedge such as brie, cut slivers lengthways. Never, ever cut the nose off a triangular wedge. Stilton is usually sliced, but if a spoon is provided, scoop a portion of cheese from the middle. Rind may be eaten or left, as you wish. Bite-sized morsels of cheese and biscuit should be brought to the mouth, rather than biting off mouthfuls from a great hunk of cheese on an entire cracker.

CHEWING

Keep your mouth closed and noise to a minimum. Never smack your chops, or talk with your mouth full. If you are required to talk, try to finish the mouthful as quickly as possible. The other person should step in and say something to fill the silence; it is equally rude for them to sit and stare at you chewing. If you're only required to say a one-word answer then you may get away with it mid-chew ... but a nod or shake of the head is also advisable. *See also Table Manners*

CHEWING GUM

The pavements of our towns and cities are splattered with gum, benches are encrusted, while the underside of school desks have their own lumpy topography – with 28 million regular chewers in Britain, the problem is still growing.

It seems clear that the fundamental breach of etiquette is not in the act of chewing but in the act of disposal. Such a cheap commodity, around in one form or another for 5,000 years (when Neolithic man chewed lumps of birch bark tar) and so popular now for reasons that range from appetite suppression to smoking deterrent to tension-easer, should not be put beyond the pale just by dint of how it is discarded. If we assume that the responsible gum-chewer knows how to get rid of it discreetly, neatly and without polluting the streets then there only remain a few basic guidelines to avoid the Non-U Chew. Chew gently, with your mouth firmly closed; determined mastication looks bovine. Blowing bubbles is for small children only. Don't swallow your gum; it is rumoured to loiter in the digestive tract, picking up other tough stuff along the way – the resulting blockages may be embarrassing to explain at the hospital.

Above all, consider adopting the Greta Garbo approach. If you must chew gum, whether to stay awake in the car, or to freshen your breath, or to stem food or nicotine cravings, then you should want 'to be alone' while doing so.

CHILDREN

'If you bungle raising your children, I don't think whatever else you do matters.'
JACQUELINE ONASSIS

For once the despairing pundits, commentators and pollsters and are in agreement: children's manners are getting worse. Table manners are a thing of the past, respect for elders is out of the window, and so on. Yet many parents riposte that it is no longer a question of manners, it's a question of natural behaviour. Their little darling may like to be louder than the town crier, may want to crawl round other people's feet in a restaurant, may need to have their parent's instant attention for their own important demands – but they're just children, and who are we to say that these natural impulses should be cramped within our own narrow view of manners?

There is clearly a disconnect here. Children are undoubtedly natural wonders, but, as Tennyson said, nature is 'red in tooth and claw'. We teach our children to walk, we teach them to talk and, if we want our children to interact successfully, we teach them manners: not just elbows-in, saying-thank-you manners, but how to rub along happily with others – both peers and those of all generations, backgrounds, abilities. The problem comes with the general lack of agreement over how to raise a well-mannered child: from the welter of parenting books to the conflicting demands and confusions of a multi-cultural society, where some children are revered as demi-gods whose will must never be contravened, while others belong to the manners-drummed-in, seen-but-not-heard camp.

Steering a middle course is clearly perilous, but there are surely some universal boundaries to be set. The parent's mantra should be, "Is my child behaving in a way that puts everyone at ease?" Never fall into the trap of imagining that your idea of 'ease' is the same as everyone else's. A child singing their favourite song over and over again can be a cute party trick at home, but in a public environment will set others' teeth on edge. Playing peekaboo for hours can be a lovely game between parent and child but don't imagine that this is the same for the stranger on a plane behind you. Table manners are not a natural attribute, they must be taught and demonstrated: watching an eight-year-old's mouth behave much like a washing machine not only puts others off their soup but shows you in a bad light.

Above all, teach by example: it's no good telling your child off for interrupting and not sitting still at the table if you then spend your next lunch party wandering around eating and shouting to make yourself heard. Do as you would be done by, as Nanny was wont to say ...

CHIVALRY

Chivalry: the courteous behaviour of a man towards a woman. But what do 'modern' women want? When is chivalry out-dated and patronising, and when is it appropriate and well-mannered? New Chivalry is all about the natural gesture, striking a balance between treating a woman like a lady, but respecting her independence. A chivalrous man will help a woman with heavy bags, offer her a seat on a train if she is elderly or pregnant, stand when she first enters a room and open the car door for her.

These are good manners that should come instinctively, rather than contrived gestures that feel outdated and oppressive. Above all, they will make women feel at ease.
See also Feminism; Politeness

CHOCOLATE

*'If some confectioners were willing
To let the shape announce the filling,
We'd encounter fewer assorted chocs,
Bitten into and returned to the box.'*
OGDEN NASH

Most people love it; many are addicted to it. The important
thing is not to look greedy around it. When you are offered
a box of chocolates, choose quickly and decisively. Don't
spend long minutes studying the guide, visibly weighing up
the pros and cons of the selection. Never dive down into the
layer underneath, leaving a handful of rejects on top for the
next person. If you are a chocaholic, restrain your impulse
to eat chocolates compulsively — it should be a private vice.

CHOPSTICKS

If your chopstick technique is unreliable and you find
yourself asking for a fork when in a restaurant it would be
a good idea to practise at home.

Hold the chopsticks parallel in one hand. Your thumb
and forefinger hold and manipulate the top stick. Your
middle finger rests between the sticks, keeping the bottom
stick held still. The top stick is manoeuvred by the thumb
and forefinger to grip food and bring it to your mouth.
Place your chopsticks by the right-hand side of your plate
when you are not using them; you may be provided with
special rests. Never use chopsticks to pass food to people,
and never use them to point at other people. *See also Sushi*

CHRISTENINGS

A church christening (known officially as baptism) welcomes
a child (or adult) into the faith of that church. Parents,
relatives, the chosen godparents and close friends attend,
and the day should be treated as a formal occasion. Non-
religious ceremonies are known as naming-parties.
Anything goes here.

Christenings often take place during a normal Sunday
service. If you aren't a regular church-goer, attempt to
engage with the whole service, and avoid looking bored or
restless. Dress smartly — jeans are not appropriate. If in
doubt, check with the child's parents. During the ceremony,
certain questions are put to the baptism party. It is advisable
to respond positively and heartily, showing your support
for the child and his/her parents.

A gift for the child may be presented to the parents.
A small, white leather-bound bible is a traditional gift, as
is silverware — such as a charm bracelet or engraved picture
frame. If you wish to go down a less traditional route, simply
ensure that the gift is a keepsake that can be treasured by the
child in the years to come. *See also Godparents; Presents*

CHRISTMAS CARDS

Choose your cards carefully. Remember that humorous
cards, or cards with religious messages inside, may not be
appreciated by everybody. It may be a good idea to buy two
sets — one for those who will enjoy a light-hearted fun card,
and another with a generic 'Season's Greetings' inside.

Email cards could be inappropriate for an elderly relative, but may be acceptable for a younger friend or colleagues.

Traditionally, the husband's name is given before his wife's, but it really is a matter of personal choice. Names should be signed with forenames included, e.g. from 'John and Mary Smith', not 'Mr and Mrs John Smith'.

It is fine to include a brief line — such as 'we must catch up in the new year' — but avoid writing an essay. Instead, you could include a short, personal letter on a separate sheet to friends or relatives who are rarely seen.

If you miss the post, or receive a last minute card from someone not on your list, then send a brief note, card or postcard with your best wishes. Alternatively, send a new year's card. It is a matter of personal choice whether you send cards at all, but remember that people who send them to you may be surprised not to receive one back.
See also Greeting Cards; Round Robins

CIVIL PARTNERSHIPS

Before the legalisation of same sex marriage, civil partnerships introduced parity, both legally and publicly, between the status of a gay couple and that of a married couple. While some people still adhere to the idea of heterosexual marriage, others see civil partnerships and same sex marriages as a joyful example of the increasing tolerance of our society.

Whatever your view, if you have been invited to a civil partnership or same sex marriage, you should consider the feelings of the couple. If you are uncomfortable with the concept, don't go – whatever your attitude, it is their day of celebration and they deserve the uncritical approval and happiness of those around them. Likewise, if you are inviting friends and family to your own civil partnership, consider the guest list carefully: you may think your elderly uncle should be there, but if he's going to be uncomfortable and awkward with your friends then perhaps he's better left off. Once accepted, the etiquette surrounding such an occasion is determined largely by the couple themselves: they will tell you how closely they are conforming to a traditional wedding day, and whether you should dress in conventional garb, throw confetti, give wedding presents, and so on.

CLEANERS

Domestic help is a billion-pound industry, as big now as it was before the Second World War, yet there is a whiff of embarrassment about this lucrative trade. We've all known friends or family who have cleaned the house before the cleaner got there, or who asked the cleaner to hide if people came round. Others refuse help altogether, saying that it is unethical to take advantage of someone else's economic misfortune by paying them peanuts to clear up our mess. Yet we are happy to use accountants, hairdressers and dentists to perform tasks that we can't do and don't have the time to do, so why should having a cleaner be any different?

Once over the hump of the decision, there are ways of ensuring that you don't get trapped in a bad cleaning

relationship. Even if you think you know, ask your new
cleaner how long it would take them to clean your house,
and if the two times are very different, negotiate a
compromise. Take the time to explain where everything
is and exactly what you want them to do on a daily/weekly/
monthly basis. You can't expect them to clean the silver and
hand-wipe each leaf of the bonsai tree if you've just waved a
hand and said airily, "You'll know what to do". Don't move
the goalposts; if you're asking them to take on more work,
you must offer them more money, it's only fair. Try not to
be embarrassed; they are seeing your life laid bare, and may
be privy to your intimate secrets – but you have to accept that
goes with the territory. Leave them to get on with the job
in peace; they will find cleaning your house much easier if
you are not following them from room, engaging them in
conversation. If their cleaning isn't up to scratch, grab the
bull by the horns, and tell them what's wrong; don't let
resentment simmer beneath the surface. Always pay on time
– and don't fuss around with presents at Christmas time:
you're not embarrassed to get a financial bonus at the end
of the year so why would they be?

CLEAVAGE

There is a fine balance between natural and indecent.
Showing too much cleavage at work may get you a reputation
rather than a rise. There are necklines for daywear and
daring plunges for evening wear. A little *décolletage* can
enhance an outfit, but sometimes less is more.

CLUBS, PRIVATE MEMBERS'
'I refuse to join any club that would have me as a member.'
GROUCHO MARX

If you have membership of a private club don't ever boast about it. If you are inviting guests, be aware that they may not know what to expect and keep them informed; are ladies permitted? Is there a dress code? Accompany them into the club or meet them at the door so you can sign them in. If you are a visitor yourself respect the club's codes of conduct. Dress appropriately and, as a general rule, don't tip the staff.

COAT, HELPING A LADY ON WITH
It is considered a courteous gesture for a man to help a lady on with her coat. Hold it up and position it so her arms can slip in easily. Lift the coat onto her shoulders as she puts her arms into the sleeves. Then lift it slightly again to make sure it settles correctly on the clothes underneath. *See also Chivalry*

COLD CALLERS
The bane of many people's existence, cold callers are an invasive nuisance, especially when their calls come during antisocial, out-of-office hours. Dealing with them, however, should never be an excuse for rudeness. Remember that they are simply doing a job, and answer them politely and firmly. Intercept their sales pitch with a courteous "I'm sorry, I'm really not interested/this is not a convenient time ..." and hang up.

COLLEAGUES

Support your workmates and they will do the same for you. If you can see someone is particularly busy or stressed there may be some way you can help without affecting your own workload too much. Always be willing to dedicate time and effort to your relationships with colleagues. This may mean giving up an evening for after work drinks or going out for lunch together once in a while.

Not all topics of conversation are suitable for office chit-chat, especially in an open plan environment, so don't embarrass your colleagues by discussing inappropriate or personal topics, and resist the temptation to gossip about other members of staff. Try to keep a balance between your work life and private life; discretion dictates that you retain some areas of privacy (and intimate personal calls at your desk are never a good idea), but it is also vital that you open up a little and find some common ground.

COMPETITIVENESS

To be competitive is both drummed into us from birth and almost as immediately decried as being rather an unattractive character trait. The achievements of our contemporaries — from potty training to A-levels — are held up as an example, but if our desire to win is too overt or overzealous we are reprimanded. Cut forward 20 years to the cut-throat years of your career and you'll find the same ambivalence. Out-performing the competition is one thing, being seen to do it in a pushy way is quite another.

One thing we have to face, even if it flies in the face of political correctness, is that, as top dog in the animal kingdom, we are naturally competitive – and that good outcomes can result from that competitiveness; as Ovid commented 2,000 years ago, 'Like man, a horse never runs so fast as when he has other horses to catch up and outpace'. Competition can raise your game – the trick is not to alienate others while you're climbing. You're not trying to knock people out as you go up the tree but build new branches of your own. No matter what the field – be it the workplace or the PTA – identify a mentor above you, find a *protégée* in the ranks below you, create a team around you as if you are linking their hands together in order for them to hoist you up to the next level. To achieve this your armoury will require plentiful supplies of two weapons: charm and knowledge. If you know what's what, who's who and here's how, then you're on the way.

COMPLAINING

Napoleon once opined, 'When people cease to complain, they cease to think'. The British love to complain, but we're not very good at it. Although we like a good whinge, we're more likely to moan at someone else than complain directly, through the proper channels or in a way that might actually fix the problem. At this moment in a restaurant near you, there is a familiar scene – a couple huddled together, comparing how salty their soup is, how cold their kedgeree, when a waiter approaches. "Everything all right here?"

"Oh yes, fine, thank you." At least this form of complaining isn't rude, because its target never gets to hear the harsh words we are having such fun delivering.

If, however, you want to complain in an effective way, there are ways and means that avoid temper, high blood pressure and shouting – never the best way to achieve your goal. Always pay lip service to calmly following the proper channels, and only when those are exhausted, do you smilingly ask if it is possible to see the manager, while making it obvious that you're not leaving until something good happens. Try if at all possible to resolve the complaint there and then rather than being fobbed off by the advice to write a letter. Remember that your adversaries are often trained in the art of 'customer service' (a.k.a. anything but) so they are skilled in complaint deflection strategies. Rudeness merely activates these strategies, whereas politeness and an eagerness to work with them to solve your problem are often disarming. Sometimes all you have to do is smile confidently and say, "I'm sure we can resolve this," or subtly remind them of the reputation they have to uphold. At all times, outdo any saccharine obtuseness with extra dollops of twice-as-nice: you will reap sweet rewards.

COMPLIMENTS

A genuine compliment will suffuse the recipient with positive feelings, and oils the wheels of social intercourse. Only offer compliments when you believe them, and don't over-compliment – you will look like an insincere flatterer.

COMPLIMENTS

Stick to specifics; vague, overgeneralised compliments
are easily devalued. Never damn with faint praise, or give
a compliment with one hand and take away with the other.
Try and give the compliment in a timely manner – don't wait
until you are leaving a dinner party to praise the food, for
example – a spontaneous response feels more genuine.

If you are the recipient of a compliment, smile and say
thank you. Don't denigrate yourself, or take it as a cue for
boasting. Never retaliate with a knee-jerk compliment back.
The recipient will, rightly, regard it with suspicion.
See also Flattery

CONVERSATION

A good conversationalist strikes a perfect balance between
talking and listening. They pick up threads to create a multi-
layered conversation and a sense of intimacy – the other
person feels sure that they are listening, and interested.

It is important to set the conversation off well. Try to
think of an alternative to the usual "How are you?" or "What
do you do?". Gentle humour, flattery and the occasional
well-placed compliment all make conversation easier.

Ask questions, but don't conduct an interview – there is
a fine line between interest and intrusion. Familiarity comes
with time, so be aware of unspoken barriers. Avoid strong
opinion or stark honesty; an occasional *frisson* is interesting,
but controversial views may offend. Never talk about money,
illness or death. Bluffers and serial liars always get their
comeuppance; name-droppers and braggers bore everyone.

COUGHING

Follow coughing etiquette: turn away from other people;
if possible cough into a handkerchief or tissue, not your
hand; if you do not have a handkerchief, cover your mouth
with your hand.

Avoid public performances – especially concerts or plays
– to avoid irritating fellow members of the audience. Ensure
you're equipped with an emergency supply of cough sweets.
If coughing is unavoidable, use other sounds to mask it
(applause, loud music, laughter).

COUNTRYSIDE RULES

Certain rules of behaviour, observed when in the country,
will ensure that you don't endanger yourself or any wildlife
during your trip. There's an age-old way of doing things in
rural Britain, so go prepared, and be aware that it's still the
norm to greet people you encounter with a friendly "Hello".

Stick to designated paths, especially in crop fields, and
when walking on a rural road, walk on the side of the road
facing oncoming traffic. When rounding a bend or blind
corner, move to the other side of the road to avoid head-
on collisions, then move back to the other side on a straight
stretch. Leave gates as you find them – they will be open
or closed for a reason. Take litter home with you if you
can't find a bin. Wild or farmland animals shouldn't be
approached, and even friendly-looking dogs on leads
should be given a wide berth, unless the owner invites
you to pet them.

CRYING

'Heaven knows we need never be ashamed of our tears, for they are rain upon the blinding dust of earth, overlying our hard hearts.'
CHARLES DICKENS

Just as the sun sets on the British Empire, so it would seem that in doing so it has melted the famously stereotypical stiff upper lip. Past guides on manners do not touch on the subject of crying because crying was simply not done, not under any circumstances except perhaps severe pain, and even then, too much blubbing would have caused a raised eyebrow or two. Now, for men and women alike, the emotional hatches have been unbattened and crying is suddenly one of life's healthier physical responses. Sportsmen are famous weepers, their manliness so epic that it cannot be diminished by a few tears. Other toughened professionals like war reporters, barristers and even the Royal Family have been known to well up.

Children cry at the drop of a hat and should never be allowed to think that crying is a short cut to instant gratification. Lachrymose adults, who cry frequently for hormonal, emotional or often purely reflex reasons, should also never be allowed to think that crying gets them what they want. Crying is forgivable under emotional duress, but many people feel uncomfortable if they have to witness tears. Tears should be suppressed if it is kinder to do so; for example when your child goes away for the first time and must not see how upset you are. Above all, crying should never be staged; the manipulative behaviour will undermine the sheer emotional release of a genuine sob.

CURTSEYING

When being introduced to a member of the Royal Family women should curtsey. To make a curtsey briefly bend your knees with one foot forward. This should again be performed when the member of the Royal Family leaves.
See also Bowing; Queen, HM The; Royal Family

CUTLERY

A knife should be held firmly in your right hand, with the handle tucked into your palm, your thumb down one side of the handle and your index finger along the top (but never touching the top of the blade). It should never be eaten off or held like a pencil.

When used with a knife or spoon, the fork should be held in the left hand, in much the same way as the knife, with the prongs facing downwards. On its own, it is held in the right hand, with the prongs facing upwards, resting on the fingers and secured with the thumb and index finger.

A spoon is held in the right hand, resting on the fingers and secured with the thumb and index finger. Food should be eaten off the side of the spoon; it should never be used at a right angle to the mouth.

Cutlery should be rested on the plate/bowl between bites, and placed together in the bottom-centre when you are finished. *See also Table Manners; Table Settings*

DANCING TO DRUNKENNESS

DANCING

As the night progresses you may think you're becoming a better dancer, but the opposite is usually true. If you've turned into a sweaty, uncoordinated muddle of flailing limbs it is time to withdraw. Equally, if you find yourself alone on the dance floor it may also be wise to exit, unless your Travolta-esque routine has drawn an admiring crowd.

If you are asked to dance and do not want to do so, refuse politely – an excuse might help to make the supplicant feel less rejected. There are certain occasions when you should make an effort to participate. If you are at a wedding or party and everyone else is dancing it would look antisocial to sit at the side. You will get lost in the crowd, so don't worry about looking foolish. If you are not confident, just keep it simple.

If you are out with one other person don't leave them sitting on the sidelines while you take to the dance floor. They may well be bored by the spectacle of you dancing or, worse still, secretly laughing.

DATING

When asking someone out on a date it is polite to do it face-to-face or at least over the phone. If you are doing the inviting it is up to you to make the arrangements. If you are going to be late give as much notice as possible, preferably by phone. Being up to 15 minutes late should not be a problem, and a brief apology will be fine. Being more than half an hour late looks perilously like rudeness unless you have a genuine excuse. Cancelling a date should be done

as far in advance as possible, and you should always phone, not email or text. If you fear you may have offended, you could send some flowers or other suitable gift.

If you have been stood up don't jump to conclusions, there may be a reasonable explanation. Make a call after about half an hour of waiting to find out what's gone wrong. If there's no answer you can suspect the worst. Maintain your dignity and don't leave an angry message. Reassure yourself that you have made a lucky escape and move on.

Conversation on a first date should centre on safe topics such as work, hobbies and family. Don't dominate the conversation but make sure you each have equal opportunity to speak. You should switch your phone onto silent and not answer calls or send text messages during the date. Paying the bill is the responsibility of the inviter, at least on the first occasion. As things progress it is fine to take turns settling the bill. It is polite for a man to ensure that his companion gets home safely – if necessary hailing her a cab. It may be convenient to share a taxi, in which case the woman should be dropped off first, unless this is impractical. If not taking a taxi, a man should accompany a woman to her bus stop/front door/station.

For a first date drinks are probably the best option, as you will not be obliged to spend the whole evening together. If things go really well you can always have dinner as well. If you have another commitment to go to afterwards tell your date at the outset. A daytime date requires spending more time together so is best left until you feel more comfortable around each other. *See also Going Dutch*

DEATH

The logistical brouhaha that surrounds a death – from
the bureaucratic nightmare of registering it to the frenzy
of the funeral arrangements – can often disguise the impact
of the death itself. In a country not known for open-casket
observances, some would say that we have lost touch with
Death. More people than ever before say they have never
even seen a dead body. Inner-city children are horrified
if they are ever reminded that the meat on their plate came
from a dead animal that once mooed or quacked. The death
of a celebrity or member of the Royal Family is treated with
an hysteria that devalues the currency of the genuine grief
felt for the death of a friend or loved one.

It is only a few steps back to the Victorian Age, with all
that era's mawkish and restrictive customs around the final
ritual, and complex sumptuary laws around appropriate
mourning ('widow's weeds'). These days we are spared such
a prohibitive – and expensive – code; but in stripping death
of its ceremonial vestments, many of us still seem at a loss
as to how to address the subject or how to treat our bereaved
friends or loved ones.

In the immediate aftermath of the death, it is often
easier; the bereaved is either concealing grief with activity
or is so steeped in misery that your presence alone is enough.
Children should not be excluded from the process or they
may feel confused and worried that the death is somehow
their fault; they don't need elaborate explanations but
merely a simple talk about beginnings and endings, with
life eternal in the form of memories.

Later on, avoid the temptation to wrap death in euphemism: when writing a letter of condolence, using terms like 'passed away' or 'moved over' merely grates. Instead aim for a frank and confiding tone, dwelling nostalgically and fondly on past happier days. The tough part of death – and grieving – is that it doesn't stop at the funeral. The best thing you can do as a friend to one who is grieving is to realise this. Support in the early days of death is a given – but maintaining those levels of support one, two, three years on is where true friendship counts.

DEPORTMENT

The way you stand, walk and sit all make a big impression. Good posture makes you appear taller and slimmer and you will seem more confident and positive.

Hold your head high, keep your back straight and pull your shoulders back. How you sit is also very important. Women should keep their knees together when seated (preferably with their ankles crossed). Men should avoid sitting with their legs excessively wide apart, and should never tap their feet or repeatedly jiggle their leg up and down. *See also Body Language*

DIAMONDS

Convention dictates that an engagement should be marked by a diamond ring. Other stones, such as sapphires and rubies, are still sometimes chosen for engagement rings, or may be used as side-setting. It is customary for the groom to pay for the ring. It is sometimes said that the ring should cost the equivalent of two months' salary, but in reality the groom should pay as much as he can afford. *See also Proposals*

DIETS

It is one of life's pure little mysteries that every woman, no matter how thin or perfect other people consider her to be, will be on a diet at some point in her life. No matter that diets (by which we mean the artificial restriction of one or more food groups) have been proven not to work in the long-term, no matter that dieting is both tedious for the dieter and exponentially more tedious for those having to hear about it, all women – and men, in increasing numbers – are conditioned to seek the Holy Grail of the perfect diet for the perfect body. So dieting is here to stay.

The appropriate response on hearing that your friend or loved one is on a diet is to offer unstinting support, constant supplies of praise and an uncritical eye – "Wow, yes, you look thinner already". In fact, your heart is probably sinking into your boots: your once entertaining friend or loved one is about to transmogrify into a bore, a human abacus of calorie-counting, a dinner party guest from hell who is going to look askance at the food you have slaved over and ask whether she can just have her chicken grilled and her vegetables steamed, if that's not too much bother? Take a deep breath, and brace yourself for the post-diet recriminations and guilt complexes.

DIETS

If you yourself are on a diet, take note of this process: never inflict your diet on others, avoid the temptation to be evangelical, never expect hostesses to cater specially for you (don't go out to dinner if you aren't prepared to fudge the issue by, say, eating only the vegetables and eschewing the calorie-bomb pudding) and never be co-conspiratorial about diets with other women. Leaning over to a fuller-figured friend and saying, *sotto voce*, "I'm doing this great diet where you eat pineapples for twelve days — I know you'd love it," is a gaffe from which you may find it hard to recover.
See also Weight, Discussing; Zero

DIGESTIFS

Alcoholic drinks served after a meal (to aid digestion) are called digestifs. Traditionally, these are strong and dark coloured drinks, such as brandy, Armagnac, cognac and whisky, or fortified wines such as port or Madeira. Sweet liqueurs are also popular choices. Postprandial indulgences are also called nightcaps. *See also Aperitifs; Port*

DINNER PARTIES

'At a dinner party one should eat wisely but not too well, and talk well but not too wisely.'
W. SOMERSET MAUGHAM

When hosting a dinner party, do as much as you can before the guests arrive. Lay the table, sort out the crockery, prepare as much food as possible — you will be able to spend more time with your guests rather than in the kitchen. Offer them a drink upon arrival. Spirits should be available as well as wine and beer. A glass of champagne is also a good option.

If someone brings a bottle you may like to open it at some point in the evening, but have your own bottle ready and opened, in case your guests don't bring wine. If you do not open your guests' wine on the night, make sure you tell them that their wine is too exceptional for the assembled group and that you're saving it for a special occasion.

A table plan is a good way of organising your guests, but can look over-formal. If you want the atmosphere to feel laid back and spontaneous, let people choose where they want to sit; just make sure that couples are separated. Keep an eye on the conversational dynamic during the first two courses; if your guests aren't meshing, suggest everyone moves round and mingles for the latter part of the evening. As host it is your duty to ensure conversation flows throughout the meal. Steer it away from topics that you know will be awkward for any of your guests.

If you have been invited to a dinner party make sure you RSVP promptly (mentioning any dietary requirements you may have). If you can't make it you'll be giving the host plenty of time to find someone else. If you have to cancel, give as much notice as possible. Never arrive early to a dinner party. A few minutes after the time stated on the invitation is polite; if you are going to be more than 15 minutes late phone ahead and warn your host.

It is polite to take a gift; chocolates, flowers, or a bottle of wine are all good choices. Take a couple of bottles if there are two of you. It is not customary to take a gift to a very formal dinner, i.e. one at which dinner jackets are worn. Always write a thank you note as soon as possible after the event. A phone call is also fine. *See also Hosts and Hostesses*

DIVORCE

'You don't know a woman till you've met her in court.'
NORMAN MAILER

It is hard to imagine introducing manners into the modern battlefield that is today's end to one in three marriages. To the two people at the centre of a divorce's maelstrom, no amount of Geneva Conventions will have any effect on the recriminations, hurt and lies that whirl around the painful end to a once-happy marriage. If taxes and death are the two certainties of life, then the process of divorce is the opposite: nothing is certain, moral high grounds will often turn out to be false summits and attempts at reconciliation will often simply draw out the agony.

If you are the one going through a divorce, you will be too miserable to pay attention to any advice from anyone, so consider yourself largely excused from any code of behaviour. Just try to consider the feelings – and long memories – of any children involved. Never, ever be tempted to confide in them; you will eventually have the maturity to recover from, and gloss over, the raw details of your marriage's collapse – but they will not. Later, much later, you will look back in amazement at the length and depth of time dedicated to self-indulgence, and at the heroic patience and endless tolerance of your friends and relatives.

As a good friend or close relative of divorcés and divorcées your limitless supply of patience and tolerance will need to be combined with a diplomat's finesse and delicacy of touch. You will also have to master the slippery art of being non-committal, which enables you to say supportive things without entirely badmouthing the ex-partner — insurance against a future reunion, when old insults are remembered with terrifying clarity and may be disinterred. Be aware of your limitations — you can probably only be truly useful as a shoulder to cry on — but also be aware of how much you are needed. *See also Ending a Relationship*

DOGGIE BAGS

The largely American habit of asking for a doggie bag in a restaurant is not widely accepted this side of the Atlantic. While a 'waste-not-want-not' attitude is admirable, you should try to finish everything on your plate. Asking for a doggie bag is likely to be viewed as a vulgar request and will raise eyebrows.

DOGS

'The most affectionate creature in the world is a wet dog.'
AMBROSE BIERCE

You may love your mutt, applaud its rambunctious barking and tolerate its messier excrescences, but you are making a big mistake if you assume the rest of the world feels the same. When you are out with your dog, keep it under control.

Be aware that small children (quite reasonably) and some adults are actually very frightened of dogs. So when your pet bounds up to strangers, puts its paws on their shoulders, barks and slobbers in their face, don't greet their antics with "He's just being friendly". Call the dog away, or drag it off, with a polite apology.

Dog mess is an intolerable nuisance, especially in the middle of pavements and paths. If you have any respect at all for your fellow human beings, you will always carry plastic bags and remove it. You may feel foolish and humiliated as you humbly clean up after your imperious, careless pet. But you have freely chosen to be a dog-owner, and that means accepting full responsibility for everything your dog does.

DOORS, HOLDING OPEN
Men holding doors open for women is still a chivalrous gesture, even in our less-gallant times. If, however, a woman arrives at the door first and starts to open it, a man shouldn't awkwardly rush in front of her exclaiming "I'll get that!". Both genders should hold doors open (and check) for people coming through behind them. *See also Chivalry*

DRESS-DOWN DAYS
Wherever you work, be assured that dress-down policy does not mean that 'anything goes': it might not apply when staff are meeting clients, and certainly won't apply on business trips abroad. Check in advance to save embarrassment.

'Smart casual' usually means the following: absolutely no sportswear, including lycra and running shoes; nothing that can be construed as beachwear, such as shorts; avoid T-shirts and sweatshirts, particularly those with logos. Check the level of informality before wearing denim. Abide by the rules of 'business casual': men should wear a shirt and collar.

If you feel more comfortable wearing a suit, there is no reason why you shouldn't. But remember that your refusal to conform to a dress-down policy may be construed negatively by an employer or by fellow colleagues. To avoid repercussions, aim for a compromise: put your suit on as normal, then do one thing to change it: for example, remove your tie, or swap your power stilettos for flats.

DRIVING

A car is a potentially lethal weapon, and a good driver will always remember this before using it as a way of expressing irritation, frustration or red-blooded rage. It goes without saying, therefore, that aggressive driving should be avoided at all costs: tailgating, with or without flashing headlights, and pointless horn-blowing are not the signs of alpha superiority, merely a dangerous inability to control emotions while in charge of a very powerful, and dangerous, machine.

Good driving manners signal a reassuring awareness of other motorists. Let other cars into the queue in front of you with a friendly wave or flash of the headlights – a graceful gesture that will only cost you seconds. Give way to oncoming traffic. Indicate when overtaking. Acknowledge other motorists' gestures – it will make crowded, frustrating roads seem infinitely more civilised. Breaking the speed limit is dangerous, but hesitant kerb-crawling can be very annoying for drivers caught behind you. If you are lost, pull over and consult a map or a passing pedestrian. If you are a passenger, never turn into a back-seat driver: you may be ashen-faced and white-knuckled with fear, but stamping on imaginary brakes and barking commands are not going to help. Lead by example, and keep calm and collected.

Be aware of other road-users. Always give cyclists plenty of leeway and slow down when approaching pedestrian crossings – if you make plenty of allowances for unpredictable behaviour you should be able to curb your antagonism, and help to make the roads a safer place.
See also Road Rage; Zebra Crossings

DRUNKENNESS

'O God, that men should put an enemy in their mouths to steal away their brains! That we should, with joy, pleasance, revel, and applause, transform ourselves into beasts!'
WILLIAM SHAKESPEARE

At the beginning of the evening, drink is the ally of social confidence; at the end of the night, it is the enemy of social manners. One minute, drinking is making you feel on top of the world, bringing a flush of excitement to your cheeks, and lending wings to your wit; the next, you've fallen over on the parquet, that flush has mottled and the amusement has stalled mid-air.

Drunkenness is not infectious; if you are drunk, you cannot rely on the discreet intoxication of those around you, and the true drunk will inevitably be regarded as a social pariah. Drink makes fools of us all, plunging us from an agreeable state of intoxicated merriment and social *bonhomie* into maudlin introspection, verbal (and occasionally physical) aggression, or neediness and over-emotionalism. We all know that moderation is the mother of good sense, that we should be happy enough with our one or two glasses of wine. Overindulgence is socially unattractive, but complete abstinence can sometimes seem antisocial and holier-than-thou.

The good news is that drinking-without-drunkenness is possible: eat well, alternate alcoholic drinks with sneaky glasses of water, never get drunker than your love interest and know your limits – the graceful drunk is always thinking beyond their immediate environment, alert to the warning signs of impending intoxication, and ready to go home before an enjoyable evening ends in tears.

If you are handling a drunk who has failed to take this path, proceed with caution. It's too late, and merely provoking, to forbid a drunk another drink: the most important thing is to stop them driving home, so call them a cab and give them their promised tipple while they're waiting. Don't bother berating them while they're still intoxicated – they won't remember it in the morning – but it's up to your conscience whether you resist the temptation to torment them with tales of their tipsiness in the morning. *See also Wagon, On the*

EATING IN PUBLIC TO **EYEBROWS**

EATING IN PUBLIC

Eating in public is not only rude (and often hypnotically revolting), it is positively bad for us. Our bodies are conditioned to fuel up when we are at rest, lolling or even reclining on the cave floor. Our morning rush is the modern-day equivalent of the primeval dawn hunt for that day's prey — for both adrenaline-kicked activities our bodies are poised in fight-or-flight mode. Eating when our bodies are tensed like this plays merry hell with our digestion, upsets our circadian rhythms and irritates our guts. Heartburn, indigestion, IBS — is this not a heavy price to pay for a quick lunch on the run? If it's our health at stake, could we perhaps pause for thought — and pause for lunch?

EAVESDROPPING

'There's nothing like eavesdropping to show you that the world outside your head is different from the world inside.'
THORNTON WILDER

Sneakily listening in to other people's private conversations is universally condemned, but everyone has succumbed to the temptation. If you must eavesdrop, just ensure that you never reveal how you've come by your information. If you are fascinated by a conversation at the next table, avoid the obvious signs of eavesdropping: cocked head, frequent glances, distracted inability to participate in your own conversation. Resist all urges to gatecrash the conversation — "Excuse me, I couldn't help but hearing ..." Your victims will, rightly, be outraged by your insouciance.

If you're an inveterate eavesdropper, it is easier, and more polite, to indulge yourself by listening in to other people's mobile phone conversations. They're going on all round you, they're frequently intimate and revealing, and the people on the phone who are loudly broadcasting their secrets don't even seem to mind you listening.

ECO-ETIQUETTE

'We could have saved the Earth but we were too damned cheap.'
KURT VONNEGUT JR.

We all know what we *should* do – the recycling, the carbon footprint, the organic foods and so on – but being eco-friendly is something that you should preferably keep between yourself and your compost bin. Proselytising is always unattractive, even when delivered with the fervour of the green-haloed. Farmers' markets, Fairtrade, 'food miles' – a self-righteous tendency to proudly broadcast your green credentials will mean you'll end up having to recycle more than just your wine bottles as your friends melt away.

On the other hand, if you're the one being preached at, then lightness of touch is the order of the day. Deflect the self-righteous superiority of your eco-critics by joking self-deprecatingly about your own green deficiencies. After all, unless you're going to get involved in a dirty, energy-intensive debate about the energy required to crush recycled bottles, the received wisdom is of course that your little green friends are in the right ...

See also Environment, Respecting; Recycling; Wasteful, Being

ELBOWS

Keep your elbows tucked into your sides when eating. Make sure that they don't encroach on the space of the person beside you. Do not lean on your elbows when eating. It is, however, fine to rest your elbows on the table when you do not have utensils in your hands. *See also Table Manners*

EMAIL

Email has replaced many traditional forms of communication, both verbal and written. The author of an email must remember that their message may be stored permanently, and that there is no such thing as confidentiality in cyberspace. Delicate communications should therefore be sent by other means, and the author must think carefully before hitting 'send' if the message is written in haste or when emotions are running high. Avoid sarcasm and subtle humour unless you know that the reader will 'get it'. If in doubt, err towards the polite and formal, particularly when you are not well acquainted with the recipient.

Aim to stick as closely as possible to the conventions of traditional letter writing. Attention should be paid to spelling and grammar, and the habit of writing in lower or upper case throughout should be avoided. A well thought-out subject line will ensure that the message gets the notice it deserves. Emails will often be printed and filed, and therefore close attention must be paid to layout. Again, treating the construction of an email just as you would a 'real' letter is the most effective approach.

Where there is more than one recipient, list them alphabetically or, in the business environment, according to hierarchy. This applies also to the 'cc' line. Avoid blind copying ('bcc') where possible: instead, forward the original email on to the third party, with a short note explaining any confidentiality. Blind copying is, however, appropriate for distribution lists, for example, where all recipients must remain anonymous.

If you send an email in error, contact the recipient immediately by telephone and ask them to ignore/delete the message. It is polite to reply to emails promptly – a simple acknowledgement with a promise that you will give the email your full attention at a given later point is preferable to 'sitting on' the message.

There is no replacement for paper and ink; in this day and age where propriety is so often sacrificed for the sake of immediacy, the truly sophisticated correspondent will put pen to paper rather than tripping out a quick email. Never use email to reply to correspondence that was not sent by email. Adhere to this rule where you are given the choice of replying by either post or email – such as an invitation where the host's email address is supplied below the RSVP address.
See also Handwritten; Punctuation

ENDING A RELATIONSHIP

There is no happy way to end a relationship, but if you can bring yourself to be direct, decisive and as kind as you think you can bear then you will stand a better chance of getting away with your dignity intact. Always meet up with your (soon-to-be-ex-) partner; email and text are a savage and brutal mode of relationship torture. Once face-to-face, do not let a hint of ambiguity weaken your case; it only looks like a chink in the armour to the desperate. Likewise, avoid being simply too nice – murmuring asinine clichés like "It's not you, it's me," will simply ensnare you in the sticky web of your own cloying half-truths. It is much better to be honest and merely regretful. Above all, don't spin out the conversation too long – the humiliation of a break-up is in its seemingly endless and protracted trotting-out of meaningless clichés.

Rejection can often have a physical effect: not just those treacherous tears but a shivery unsteadiness. Another relationship will seem unimaginably distant. The first thing to do is to write a list of your ex's shortcomings. Soon the list will fade into irrevelance, as your memory of the pain of the break-up diminishes. You know you have finally moved on when you find your own misery boring. Then the relationship has truly ended – for both of you. *See also Divorce*

ENGAGEMENT

It is usual for a newly engaged couple to tell the happy news to their parents first; they should then spread the word to friends and colleagues. The engagement may then be announced publicly in the 'Forthcoming Marriages' column of a local or national newspaper. This should be organised by the bride's parents. Wording should read:

Mr P Jennings and Miss K Ashton-Smythe
The engagement is announced between Peter, second son of Mr and Mrs
Simon Jennings of Lewes, East Sussex, and Katherine, only daughter
of Mr and Mrs John Ashton-Smythe of Godalming, Surrey.

In days gone by, the mother of the groom-to-be wrote to the bride-to-be's parents, expressing her happiness at the engagement. Nowadays, this is not necessary, but a written exchange between the two families is recommended.

Once the engagement is made public, friends should send a letter or card of congratulations. The letter should be addressed either to the bride-to-be or her fiancé but never jointly, even if they are living together — well-wishers should write to the person who is their relation or original friend.

Many couples will celebrate with an engagement party: anything from a small dinner party given by the bride-to-be's parents, to a larger party for family and friends hosted by both sets of parents, or a drinks party hosted by the couple themselves. The bride-to-be's father, if he is a host of a party, should make an informal speech and toast the couple. Presents are not expected, but a small token is a nice gesture. All guests should write thank you letters to the host.

If an engagement is called off, there is usually no need for a detailed explanation. Some families — perhaps if they are particularly well-known or well-connected — issue a public announcement. The wording should simply read:
The marriage arranged between Mr Peter Jennings and Miss Kate Ashton-Smythe will not take place.

If wedding invitations have already been sent out, informal notes or printed cards should be sent to each guest announcing that the ceremony will not take place. The engagement ring and any presents the former bride-to-be has given her fiancé should be returned. Any wedding presents received should be returned with a letter of thanks. *See also Diamonds; Presents; Proposals; Marriage*

ENTRANCES

While you may want your arrival at a social event to be duly noted, don't act like a drama queen. Interrupting an interesting conversation, boldly buttonholing the guest of honour, or making an obvious beeline for the drinks or food will only cause raised eyebrows. Loitering, wallflower-like, and waiting to be noticed can be equally annoying. Walk in confidently and make yourself known immediately to the host and hostess. Take time to assess the ambience of the event before launching yourself into the social maelstrom. *See also Exits*

ENVELOPES

Handwrite envelopes for personal correspondence in ink. Titles and decorations should be written out in full.

Personal letters should be sent in diamond-flapped envelopes that match the writing paper. Always use a stamp (stuck straight) – never a franking machine – at home. Brown envelopes, A4 printer-type paper and envelopes with flat flaps are only suitable for office use, not personal correspondence. *See also Letter Writing*

ENVIRONMENT, RESPECTING

Small, beneficial changes to day-to-day behaviour soon
evolve into accepted practices and become the norm.

Opt for low-energy light bulbs, and ensure that you have
loft insulation and cavity wall insulation. Switch to Green
Energy suppliers. Buy organic goods, minimising 'food
miles'. Eschew products that use excessive packaging:
bring your own carrier bags when you shop. Reduce your
contribution to landfill by using recycling and composting
facilities. Donate unwanted goods to second-hand shops.

Leave the car at home and try walking, cycling or public
transport. When replacing your car, look for the most
carbon efficient. Choose a carbon neutral airline and you
will play your part in lessening the negative effects of travel.
You know it makes sense, but resist the temptation to
preach to the unconverted... *See also Eco-Etiquette; Recycling*

EVENINGWEAR

The dress code for an evening occasion will usually be
specified as white tie, black tie or, less frequently, lounge
suits. White tie is the most glamorous and formal, and
is usually reserved for state banquets and ambassadorial
functions. Ladies would usually be expected to wear a ball
gown. Black tie can be used to describe formal evening dress
generally, but it requires a black dinner suit with a white
dress shirt and black bow tie. For ladies, a cocktail dress
(long or short) is appropriate. 'Lounge suits' is less formal,
but a suit, shirt and tie are still expected. *See also Black Tie*

EXCUSES

'I attribute my success to this: I never gave or took an excuse.'
FLORENCE NIGHTINGALE

We live in a world padded out with meaningless excuses that merely muffle and annoy. Leaves on the line, the wrong sort of snow, the ubiquitous signal failure – transport excuses alone have soured us all into total cynics . . . .

If you are the person attempting to dodge something or someone, making excuses can often seem the polite way out. You don't want to tell someone you don't want to meet them, or help them out, or come to their charity evening – because to do so would be rude – so you make an excuse. The trouble is that you are then trapped by the excuse: do you hide in your house until it's safe to come out? Is it not better to examine why you're making the excuse in the first place? Is it not then kinder to avoid making excuses and stick more closely to the truth? The truth may sound bald and unadorned, but you won't have to remember which excuse you made the next time you see the inviter. Excuses will change into a complex web of lies all too easily.

If you are truly stuck with having to make an excuse (because you might get sacked from work, or dropped by a friend or lover) then the key is to stick to the truth as far as possible, keep it simple, involve no one else and then tell as few people as possible. As for making excuses about your own behaviour, this is best avoided. Benjamin Disraeli's famous comment, 'Never complain and never explain,' was all about strength, confidence and knowing when to stop talking. Excusing yourself only dilutes that strength.

EXES

'Experience is the name everyone gives to his mistakes.'
WOODROW WILSON

Good behaviour is paramount when dealing with your ex.
Revenge tactics or bad-mouthing will only make you look
bitter. If you bump into your ex be polite and cheerful,
and if you find the encounter painful, make your excuses
and leave. When meeting your partner's ex, mature good
manners are the best policy. Don't make scathing comments
to your partner about their ex; you'll appear insecure.

If you wish to maintain good relations with your ex, you
will have to accept and be friendly towards their new partner.
Be completely honest with your current partner; they will
need reassurance that no feelings remain between you.
Group meetings are best when dealing with exes; constant
one-to-ones are never going to look innocent.

EXITS

Leave decisively: don't loiter in the hallway, coat on,
prevaricating. Once you've decided to leave, say your
goodbyes to other guests, and then thank your host or
hostess before heading for the door. Try not to disrupt
other guests' enjoyment. If you are leaving mid-event, make
your departure swift and discreet, ensuring that you do not
precipitate the end of the party. If you are the last person
left, and your hosts are visibly wilting, you have probably
outstayed your welcome. Now is the time to make your exit.
See also Entrances

EYE CONTACT

Modern manners would seem to dictate that eye contact
is a 'good thing'. Jobseekers are taught to maintain firm
eye contact with their interviewers; children are exhorted
to look someone in the eye if they speak to them; blind-
daters are lectured about the necessity to gaze at their
opposite number; everyone agrees that catching a barman's
eye is the best way to get served.

But as with most diktats, it's best not to go too far with
eye contact. In a sauna, shower or other gym situation, eye
contact with anything other than the wall or your own navel
is construed at best as a come-on, at worst as an affront.
If you're so obsessed with maintaining eye contact in an
interview or on a date that you actually forget to maintain
the conversation, then any good will be undone.

Remember that there's a mere blink between gazing and
staring. Staring is never good. To a drunk, the tiniest glance
can seem like aggressive staring, so avoid eye contact in such
situations. Catching someone's eye on a train, in a bar or in
the park can be interpreted as an invitation to conversation
whether you like it or not, so prepare for the consequences.
Children choose to have eye contact with those they trust —
perhaps that isn't such a bad lesson for all of us.

EYEBROWS

Keep eyebrows trimmed. Hairy caterpillars and bushy
monobrows are not a good look on anyone. Women should
also avoid startled over-plucking.

FACIAL EXPRESSIONS TO FUNERALS

FACIAL EXPRESSIONS

The stereotype of the British stiff upper lip has traditionally paralysed our attitude towards expressing visible emotion. Empire was built on the deadpan, the clenched jaw, the occasional polite smile. But of late, we have begun to relax our faces (those of us, at least, who have resisted the frozen allure of Botox). After all, we don't need to bluff our way through life, poker-faced; we all know it's a rollercoaster of emotional highs and lows. In fact, there now seems to be a trend for extravagant facial expressions, from the gurning, eye-widening and jaw-dropping of the TV talent competition and morning chat shows to the fake shark's grin of the salesman.

Never forget, however, the simple power of the small facial gesture; lifting an eyebrow to express everything from contempt to conspiratorialism, pursing one's lips to suggest disapproval – these are minute movements that can crush or uplift those around you.

FAILURE

'I haven't failed. I've just found ten thousand ways that don't work.'
THOMAS EDISON

Failure is becoming more fashionable, a side-effect of the growing tendency to nurture ambitions that outstrip talents. While failure can clearly be something black and white – missing a target at work, getting fired, not passing an exam – more often it is about not living up to our own (unreasonable) benchmarks of success. Our children are protected from

FAILURE

failure. In schools the emphasis is on positive affirmation and competitions where everyone is a winner. While this spares children from routine humiliation, it also leaves them woefully ill-prepared for harsh reality.

Failure happens: and you will react to it far more kindly in others and in yourself if you recognise the fatefulness of many failures. *Schadenfreude*, the malicious enjoyment of others' failure (while sometimes tempting), is unworthy of you. Passing judgement on someone because they have failed at something doesn't advance the sum of human happiness – it is neither motivating enough to help them succeed next time nor retrospectively useful. Looking back at all your actions and analysing your failure is certainly the modern way, but do you really need to turn therapist and examine the roots of failure? As W.C. Fields said so forcefully, 'If at first you don't succeed, try, try again. Then quit. No use being a damn fool about it'. What is important is that you are merely better placed to avoid failure next time. Moreover, the ability to fail gracefully stands us in greater stead than an unattractive hunger to succeed every time.

FAKE TAN

Trust your fake tan to the professionals; orange knees, streaks and bronzed palms are just some of the hazards of amateur fake tanning. Ask your friends if they think you're overdoing it. Some people don't know when to stop, but it would be the height of bad manners to point this out.

FASHION

'Every generation laughs at the old fashions, but follows religiously the new.'
HENRY DAVID THOREAU

Whilst strict rules of dress disappeared with the burning of bras in the 1960s, today's fashion etiquette revolves not around rigid, restrictive do's and don'ts, but around the golden rule of propriety: always dress appropriately for the occasion. If in doubt about what to wear for a function, ask someone who is personally involved. Fashion is no longer prescriptive: it is not about what 'goes together' – if it feels good to you, you're probably doing something right.

Don't fall into the trap of becoming a fashion snob, particularly when it comes to labels. There's a fine line between looking stylish and looking like a fashion victim. The key to fashion is allowing one's eye to adjust to what's new and applying it carefully to one's own look, rather than slavishly buying the latest creations that appear on the catwalks of Milan (which may be entirely inappropriate for your age or figure) or, worse, lingering in a fashion rut.

FAUX PAS

'If I could drop dead right now, I'd be the happiest man alive.'
SAMUEL GOLDWYN

Whether it's asking someone when they're due when they're not actually pregnant, or commiserating with a colleague on his redundancy when he doesn't even know he's about to be fired, there are *faux pas* lurking at every turn. *Faux pas* are inevitable, but it's how you react to one or recover from committing one that dictates whether it will then become a harmless anecdote or a fiery brand of shame.

If someone puts their foot in it with you, the temptation is to be British and polite — a tinkling laugh and a brushing-off the "When is it due?" question, for example. But the offender is well aware that you are just putting a brave face on their rudeness, which makes them feel worse. Better all round is to make a joke about their *faux pas*, answering, "No, I'm just hugely fat." First, it gently mocks them for asking such an absurd and dangerous question, while also implying that you really don't care what they think, thereby letting them off the hook for the *faux pas* in the first place. Likewise, if you are the one making the gaffe, apologising profusely merely invites your audience to give you a spade to help you dig deeper. Never be defensive; as Eleanor Roosevelt scorned, 'No one can humiliate you without your own consent'. Self-deprecation will lighten the mood and always makes other people feel better. Admit that you're a tactless oaf, make a joke of it. Take comfort from the fact that you are not alone and that, handled deftly, this can become an amusing story for both you and your victim.

FEMINISM

'Women who seek to be equal with men lack ambition.'
TIMOTHY LEARY

The rise of the poised modern woman, able to pay for her own meals, carry her own bags and open a door for her male colleagues, or the emergence of the proud stay-at-home mum with her hard-won work-life balance, has levelled the feminist playing field when it comes to etiquette. Women no longer *need* to have the door opened, and are no longer threatened by a man who does so.

Everyone, male or female, deserves to be treated with respect and consideration. The modern feminist wouldn't think twice about helping a male colleague carry a heavy armload of files: it isn't a Man struggling to lift them, it is a Person. Likewise, modern men know that just because a woman likes to dress in a high-heeled feminine way doesn't mean that she is a) asking for it b) using her sexuality to advance herself or c) preparing to hook her man and become the little housewife. Most young people expect that their female peers will do at least as well as their male counterparts in their careers. Older, more cynical, citizens know that it's not quite this easy: there are still glass ceilings, familial pressures and other battles to be won but the fight is no longer over etiquette — we all applaud good manners.
See also Chivalry; Sexism; Wiles, Feminine

FINGER BOWLS

Finger bowls are small bowls containing water and a slice of lemon, or sometimes a flower or petal. They are usually provided if your food is to be eaten with your fingers and if any shelling is required, such as prawns. Dip your fingers in the bowl one hand at a time, rub gently to remove any stickiness and then dry them on your napkin.

FIRST IMPRESSIONS

To make a good, and lasting, first impression, always focus
on other people; do not strive to make yourself the centre
of attention. Listen carefully and make direct eye contact.
Speak clearly, and respond immediately to what is being
said. Ask questions, and listen to the answers. Try hard to
remember the name of the person you have been introduced
to, and use it at least once (overuse can look smarmy).

FIRST NAMES, USE OF

The use – or not – of first names is generational; the older
you are, the more you think it natural to be Mr, Mrs or Miss;
the younger you are, the more unimaginable this seems.
At some point in the middle, you come to expect your title
and surname in your dealings with professional people:
when seeing a doctor, a lawyer or the head-teacher at your
child's school. But there's a struggle for many in being
called Mrs X by their cleaner or by their children's friends
because of the automatic formality that it seems to generate.

The use of first names is meant to imply intimacy but this
has become a cheapened currency when used, for example,
by waiters. "Hello-my-name-is-Terry-what-can-I-get-
for-you-this-evening?" trotted out in a monotone, actively
puts a distance between you and him. Cheaper still is the
catch-all 'darling' or 'mate' of modern parlance, which
is often just a lazy way of avoiding the first name/surname
issue altogether. Don't confuse natural courtesy with the
packaged, processed wholesale adoption of over-familiarity:

waiters, call centre operatives and salesmen are not aiming
to be your friends, so why are they telling you their first
names and calling you by yours?

The curmudgeonly might argue that there has been a
breakdown of respect in our society – but perhaps we should
applaud the increasing lack of empty formalities. Surely it is
better to have agreeable manners and call someone by their
first name, than be rude to someone while rigidly adhering
to correct form and using their surname? *See also Informality*

FISH, EATING

Fish on the bone is not something to be tackled by the
uninitiated unless you are in forgiving company. Work down
one side of the spine at a time, from head-end to tail-end.
Ease mouthful-sized pieces from the fish. Never flip the
fish over to reach the underside flesh – lift the bone up and
gently ease the flesh out from beneath. Small bones should
be removed from the mouth with fingers and placed on the
side of the plate. When in doubt, order a fillet. In some
better restaurants the waiter will fillet the fish for you *à table*.
See also Caviar; Lobster; Mussels; Oysters; Prawns; Sushi

FLATMATES

Living with friends or acquaintances brings with it a
minefield of checks and balances. Set the ground rules:
how will bills be split? Are the milk and butter communal?
How is the house going to stay clean and tidy? Consider

a housework rota, or employ a cleaner. Your bedroom is yours to treat as you wish, but communal areas should be tidy and free from your detritus. Respect your flatmates' privacy; always ask before you borrow clothes, CDs, etc. Spending too long in the bathroom or on the phone may result in strained relations, so keep an eye on the clock.

FLATTERY

'Flattery is all right as long as you don't inhale.'
ADLAI STEVENSON

Assuring a friend that, yes, her diet has really worked when you know she's feeling low in the self-esteem stakes is kind; flattering your boss that he or she is a great manager is purely common sense; being flattered by your partner, whether alone or in front of others, brings a cosy glow for all.

But for flattery to work its inoffensive magic, the person being flattered must be entirely aware of the nature of the spell. Hence the social contract: Flatterer A pays Recipient B the favour of a little harmless flattery. Recipient B returns the favour by not taking it all too seriously. Both A and B feel happy, without recourse to irrevocable statements or harmful lies. Just don't ever believe the propaganda.

Of course it would be better to live in a world where compliments finally ousted flattery for ever – compliments are real, flattery is fake. But if we didn't have the easy art of flattery, the difficult art of complimenting without then sounding fake would be even more fraught with difficulties – and life is already difficult enough. *See also Compliments*

FLIRTING

'God created the flirt as soon as he made the fool.'
VICTOR HUGO

There are two types of flirting: social and romantic.
Social flirting helps the world go round. There are many
situations (work do's, parties) where some light, enjoyable
flirting, with someone you have no romantic interest in,
is appropriate. Successful social flirts put those around
them at ease; they recognise the line between fun and sleaze.

Romantic flirting has a purpose. A background
information check is essential – is your target single,
married, is your best friend also interested? A few secret
smiles and some careful eye contact (no staring) is a good
starting point. Conversation should be kept fun and light,
with the opportunity to include a few teases and gentle
physical contact (a touch of the arm, a light nudge).
Successful romantic flirts recognise when to stop and move
on, but they also know how to leave someone wanting more.

Flirting is all about being appropriate. Never flirt with
your best friend's other half, or your partner's best friend/
brother/sister/mother/father. Men should remember that
flirting is subtle; wolf whistling, shouting to get attention
or bottom pinching doesn't count. *See also Seduction, Art of*

FLOWERS

Flowers are incredibly versatile. They are the perfect
impromptu present, an appropriate gesture to acknowledge
a very happy, special or sad occasion, and they can seal the

deal when trying to impress a woman. If you have let
a woman down or fear you have offended her in some
way, flowers may say more than an embarrassed apology.
Be prepared to spend, and don't economise. Never buy
bunches from the supermarket or garage. Don't overlook
the importance of the card that accompanies a delivered
bouquet — it is an important part of the present.

Make sure the bouquet suits the occasion and the style
of the recipient (e.g. classic or contemporary). Avoid white
flowers for celebratory bunches (they are often associated
with funerals and death). Mixed bouquets can look cheap
if they aren't substantial and well-styled; instead, consider
buying a bunch of all one type of bloom or going for just a
single colour. Utilise greenery — it can bulk up the bouquet
and complement the flowers — and pick seasonal blooms,
which will be better value and in better condition.

FOREIGN OBJECTS IN FOOD

You may be unlucky enough to find a slug in your lettuce,
a fly in your soup or even something unidentifiable in your
meal. If you are in a restaurant, alert the waiter, or manager,
who should be happy to change your meal. If you are eating
at someone's house play it down; your friend will feel bad
enough without you making things worse.

If you unknowingly put the foreign object in your mouth,
remove it discreetly by bringing your fork to your mouth,
placing the offending item on it and lowering it to the side
of your plate.

FOREIGN TRAVEL

Abiding by foreign customs while travelling is both the least
you can do and the hardest thing to achieve. Whether it's
showing the soles of your feet in Thailand, leaning up
against a Maori table in New Zealand or eating with your left
hand in India, the pitfalls and pratfalls are too numerous to
mention. The basic rules are obvious: do read that boring
bit at the beginning of the guide book about customs and
etiquette in your chosen destination; err on the side of
caution when it comes to revealing clothing, and keep your
eyes peeled for how those around you are behaving. If the
monks around you are silent when you visit a Buddhist
temple, follow their lead; or, at the other end of the
politeness spectrum, if you're trying to get bus tickets at
a bus station, don't waste time queuing politely in a line
if the locals are scrummaging in a free-for-all. Adapt the
usual maxim and do as you can see others are being done by.

Try to resist the closed attitude of thinking that your
way is the right way, and above all, avoid the arrogance of
imagining that everyone on your travels speaks English –
or should do. A good starting-point is to have some
humility about your own inability to speak anything
in their language beyond "How much is this?".

Always bear in mind Mark Twain's observation, 'I have
found that there ain't no surer way to find out whether
you like people or hate them than to travel with them'.
Travelling with even your greatest friend or lover can place
unexpected strains on the relationship, largely avoided if
you adhere even more scrupulously than usual to the rules

of living together. Little things like keeping yourself tidy and clean, sticking to joint plans, making sure you're as punctual as possible, adhering to an agreed budget — these tiny observances can make or break your travelling experience.

FORGETTING NAMES

'Men are men; the best sometimes forget.'
WILLIAM SHAKESPEARE

Remembering the names of people you have been introduced to can be a haphazard business. Some names are unusual, absurdly inappropriate, comic or pretentious, and will therefore stick in your mind. Many names are instantly forgettable, and more drastic measures need to be taken. Using the name a couple of times in conversation soon after you've first heard it might fix it in your memory (but don't overdo this, or you'll sound like an importunate salesman). Try visualisation techniques; for example as soon as you hear the name, mentally blazon it across the person's forehead. Or try a mnemonic; think of something memorable that rhymes with the name, for example. Above all, don't become so obsessed with remembering the name that you fail to participate in the conversation.

If you do forget, don't panic — you can generally negotiate your way through a conversation without naming names, and you can always find out later. If all else fails, a charming and self-deprecating "I'm so sorry, I'm terrible at remembering names, I always do this ..." should dig you out of the hole. *See also Introductions*

FORMAL DINNERS

Formal dinners are still common in the armed forces,
at some universities and in the Inns of Court. Bound
up in ritual and tradition, they can be daunting for the
uninitiated. It is the responsibility of the person who
has invited you to brief you on what you should expect.

You should arrive on time and dress appropriately,
following the dress code on your invitation. Look
particularly to the top table for cues as to when to sit down,
start eating, leave the table etc. Refrain from leaving the
table during dinner. Table manners should be faultless;
this really is the time to be on your best behaviour.

Be prepared for speeches and toasts. Don't finish
everything in your glass and find yourself with nothing
to raise a toast with. If the National Anthem is played you
should be upstanding, leaving your glass on the table until
the end. If the Loyal Toast is offered simply stand and repeat
'The Queen' after the principal host. Speeches and port
follow the toasts. *See also Loyal Toasts; Port Etiquette; Speeches*

FRIENDSHIP

'Truth springs from argument amongst friends.'
DAVID HUME

The advice on how to be a good friend could be summed
up in one word: listen. Your job as a friend is to be there
when needed, at all times and in all scenarios — as comedian
Milton Berle commented, 'Friends help you move. Real
friends help you move bodies'.

It is useful to understand both the passive and active parts that go into the high-octane cocktail of true amity. Passively, you listen, comfort, support; you know not to give direct advice but merely reflect back a slightly tweaked version of their own view. You always turn up at their birthday parties, bail them out of boring situations at other people's parties, you act as alibi or frontman in complicated situations, you are unstinting in your generosity in lending clothes, money and time. You resist the inevitable envy when your friend tops you on the love, career, and looks front. Actively, you know when to cross into the dangerous territory of saying something to your friend that no one else can (whether it's about their bad behaviour or their bad taste); you can anticipate their needs without them having to ask for your help every time; you positively avoid flirting with their partner. Sometimes you will have to be a good friend even when you don't quite agree with the friend's point of view. You may fall out with your friend, but you will manage this so that it's a good clean blowout, not a festering boil of resentment that is far more painful to lance.

Never make the mistake of merely neglecting a good friendship; no matter how tried and tested, it is still a plant that needs watering. We are probably ruder to our good friends than to anyone else: social niceties are deemed superfluous, but friendships can be surprisingly fragile.

If you are obeying all these strictures, the least you can expect is the same in return. Sometimes, the hardest thing is recognising that a friendship is not truly reciprocal, and ending it. *See also Overfamiliarity*

FUNERALS

A funeral service is open to the public, unless the family
of the deceased request that it be a private ceremony. When
attending a funeral, dress sombrely. Men should wear a dark
suit with a white shirt and dark tie. Women might choose not
to wear black, but should opt for similarly subdued colours
and simple, clean lines. If a hat is worn, it should not draw
attention to the wearer. Dress with an eye to the weather,
remembering that churches and cemeteries can be cold,
even in the height of summer.

The practical elements of a funeral can vary according to
local tradition and the family's desires. Often the mourners
take their place in the church before the coffin is brought
in, which is followed by close family. In a crematorium the
mourners may follow the family into the building, after the
coffin. Whatever the venue, the front right-hand seats are
reserved for the family, with the chief mourner sitting on
the end of the front row, nearest the coffin.

Follow requests regarding funeral flowers carefully –
many families specify that flowers should not be sent, or
that a charitable donation is preferred. Where flowers are
appropriate, choose a tasteful spray or a wreath. Pure white
is considered the most fitting colour, though sending
particular flowers that are known to have been a favourite
of the deceased is a touching personal gesture. The
accompanying card should be addressed to the deceased,
not the family, and should bear a message of memorial, not
of sympathy. The classic message reads 'In loving memory'.
Flowers should be sent directly to the undertaker.

GAMESMANSHIP TO GYM ETIQUETTE

GAMESMANSHIP

'Win as if you were used to it, lose as if you enjoyed it for a change.'
RAPLPH WALDO EMERSON

This can be defined as the art of winning unfairly at
sport without actually cheating. If a player profits from
an unfair advantage, or covers up an unjust act, or
intimidates his opponent/s by words or body language
he is guilty of gamesmanship, which is the antithesis of
good sportsmanship. Unfortunately, histrionic questioning
of line calls, hectoring and haranguing referees/umpires
and taunting and goading opponents permeate all levels
of professional sport, from tennis to football. It is scarcely
surprising, therefore, that amateurs are aping the less
attractive attitudes of the professionals, and bending the
rules in order to win.

Any tendency to employ these tactics should be
eradicated. Good manners in sport are paramount, as
in other aspects of life. Even if this means you lose again
and again, at least you will be doing it gracefully.
See also Sportsmanship

GARLIC

Consider those around you when it comes to garlic. If you
are cooking for others be careful not to overpower the food
with garlic – it is a strong taste, which your guests may not
share. If you are going to be in close contact with others after
eating garlic, bear in mind that they will be able to smell
strong garlic on your breath, even if you can't.

GODPARENTS

A child traditionally has three godparents: a boy has two godfathers and one godmother, and a girl has two godmothers and one godfather. While tradition also dictates that a godparent is expected to become the legal guardian of the child should anything happen to the parents, this scenario is unlikely today. If this is the intention, the parents should make a formal statement of their wishes in their wills.

Careful thought should go into both choosing godparents and considering whether to accept the role. Being asked to be a child's godparent is a huge honour. Before accepting, ask yourself honestly whether you are prepared and able to fulfill the role. Try to understand what the parents want from you. You must be ready and willing to have regular contact with the family: don't enter into this relationship knowing that you will be one of those godparents who no one has seen for years.

Ask yourself why you were asked to be a godparent in the first place — what makes you different from the parents and other godparents: culture, glamour, sporting prowess, sociability? Play up to that reason. As godparent, you can be in the uniquely gratifying position of being the child's first grown-up friend and confidant. Treat them as your equal, and never judge or nag your godchild. Make yourself accessible; when they're old enough, give the child your mobile number and let them know that they always can call you for a chat. Never, ever forget a birthday or Christmas. Send postcards from holidays; always let them know that they are in your thoughts. *See also Christenings*

GOING DUTCH

'Going Dutch' is not recommended on a date. Instead, the person who issued the invitation should pick up the tab. More established couples should take it in turns if they are financially equal. Groups of friends should 'Go Dutch' and split the bill equally. *See also Bill, Paying the; Dating*

GOSSIP

'It is perfectly monstrous the way people go about nowadays, saying things against one, behind one's back, that are absolutely and entirely true.'
OSCAR WILDE

Humans are predisposed to gossip: we know we shouldn't repeat scandalous stories, or pass on personal anecdotes to a wider audience or take public enjoyment from someone else's misfortunes, but we also know that not all gossip is toxic. We owe much of our knowledge of our human history to the written gossip of correspondents down the millennia. Gossip is an important information exchange, an efficient means of defining what is (and isn't) socially acceptable and often serves as a useful vent for anger that might otherwise erupt into real conflict.

We gossip about others in the tacit acceptance that they might well therefore be gossiping about us. As Oscar Wilde said, 'There is only one thing in the world worse than being talked about, and that is not being talked about'. Part of the fun of gossip lies in the danger; being overheard is a real risk so watch your back. If you realise that you've been overheard

spilling secrets, you can either pursue the risky policy of apologising (the right thing to do if you've actually been caught bad-mouthing someone) or you can bluff it out and pretend you never knew it was top-secret material.

If you overhear some gossip about yourself, it is tempting to let the guilty parties dig their own grave by allowing them to rant and then letting them know you heard everything. Avoid this temptation; it will leave a nasty taste in the mouth for all concerned. Avoid righteous indignation if the gossip that you overhear is actually the truth (but an uncomfortable truth that you were reluctant to confront). *See also Whispering*

GRACE, SAYING

Some households observe the tradition of pausing before a meal to give thanks for the food on the table and other blessings in their lives. Always be prepared for this to happen. A sensitive host will not expect you to join in, and you should not feel bound to do so, particularly if you do not subscribe to the particular religion, but you must behave respectfully. Simply bowing your head and closing your eyes while the prayer is said will suffice.

GRAMMAR

In an age when instant communication is key, and text messages and emails are littered with abbreviations and verbless sentences, it seems impossibly old-fashioned to insist on good grammar. But even in a world of immediate messaging, grammar is important because it clarifies thought and removes ambiguity. If you want to be understood, then take time to think about punctuation, verb agreement, syntax and spelling – recipients will appreciate the clarity of your writing. Use spell-checkers discriminatingly; they are not 100 per cent reliable, as they do not check the context in which you use the words. Remember: no one was ever lampooned for writing well.

GRAPES
Do not pick individual grapes off a bunch. Use your fingers, or grape scissors, to remove a small bunch.

GREETING CARDS
Greeting cards can be used for a multiplicity of occasions, from birthdays to congratulations to thank-yous. But always remember one rule: do not use a greeting card to articulate an emotion that you cannot verbalise yourself. It is always inappropriate, for example, to send a 'With Deepest Condolences' card to someone who is suffering a bereavement; a handwritten, personal note is infinitely more meaningful. It is much better to write a personal note of thanks to a hostess; alternatively you can write a message inside a blank card. If you do choose a card with a customised greeting, ensure that it is appropriate to the occasion and the recipient – be especially careful around the more *risqué* messages. *See also Christmas Cards*

GUEST LIST

Those with friends in high places can fast-track themselves to the other side of the velvet rope in a nanosecond; if you are lucky enough to be on the list, never shout your name or make a song and dance about your elevated status. If there's 'been a mistake' never try the 'don't you know who I am' trick. Desperation is unlikely to get you VIP treatment.

GUESTS, HOUSE

Some people are the perfect house guests. They arrive on time, bearing carefully-chosen gifts, regale you with amusing anecdotes, wash-up, make their own beds and leave early in the morning. Others invite themselves, come late (or early), only remember to warn you of their food intolerances as you're putting plates of lovingly-prepared but unsuitable food in front of them, loll nonchalantly — while drinking your best wine and boring on about their lives — as you clear up around them, and leave their room looking like a bomb site. The difference between the paragon and the pest is that with the former, your only memory of their visit is of laughter and entertainment, and with the latter, you're working to erase both the physical detritus and your feelings of irritation for days afterwards.

The true house guest from hell, however, is the one that does all of the above and then doesn't know when to leave. As the expression goes, 'visitors, like fish, stink in three days'. If you are the visitor, follow an easy code of behaviour to avoid forever queering your pitch with hospitable friends.

Confirm both times of arrival and times of departure well before you're due to show up. Bring a present, not necessarily flashy, but thoughtful – for example, a single-malt if you know it's their particular tipple. Keep the physical evidence of your presence in their house to a minimum and tidy up after yourself. Above all, leave exactly when you said you would: too early and it looks like you're trying to escape, too late and you've outstayed your welcome. Once you're home, send a handwritten note thanking your hosts for their hospitality.

If you're the welcoming host, you will deserve to have this perfect house guest if you do your bit – putting flowers into a tidy spare room with fresh sheets and not making too big a deal about cooking extra meals. Don't be a martyr, accept offers of help, and resist the urge to celebrate as soon as their car is out of sight – just in case they forget their wellies and turn back ... *See also Visitors, Unexpected*

GYM ETIQUETTE

Wear clean, presentable gym clothes and deodorant when working out. Carry a towel with you and try to keep sweat off the machines. Wipe equipment down when you have finished with it. Don't swoop immediately on just-vacated equipment; the user may be resting between repetitions. Don't offer advice on other people's workouts and don't stare at fellow gym-goers. If wearing headphones, keep your music at a volume inaudible to others, and ensure that others are not watching the TV before changing channels.

HAIR to HYPOCHONDRIA

HAIR

Hair should be kept clean and free from dandruff. Do not brush it or play with it at the table or near food. Avoid constant fiddling and twirling and never put it in your mouth. Try not to scratch your head fiercely in public.

If you find a hair in your food when eating out, discreetly place it on the side of your plate and refrain from making a huge fuss. If you feel sufficiently unhappy, signal for the waiter to change your meal. If you are at someone's house try and resume eating once you've removed the hair.

HANDKERCHIEFS

The handkerchief is a dying object, regarded more as a decorative adornment peeking out of a gentleman's breast pocket than as an essential item. If you have a streaming cold, it is best to opt for disposable tissues.

Under no circumstances should you offer to lend a handkerchief to someone unless it is perfectly clean and unused. If you are lent a handkerchief to dry tears or relieve a runny nose, do not give it back to the owner immediately. Launder it and return it at a later date. *See also Nose Blowing*

HANDSHAKES

A firm handshake, lasting a few seconds, is the common form of greeting for all business situations and most social situations too. Always use your right hand, and 'pump' the hand two or three times before you let it go. Ensure that your fingers grip the other person's palm, otherwise you will crush their fingers. Be careful not to clench in a bone-crushing grip, but do not offer a limp hand. Check that your palms are not sweaty or clammy before shaking hands.

HANDWRITTEN

'Poets don't draw. They unravel their handwriting and then tie it up again, but differently.'
JEAN COCTEAU

Just like the demise of the book, the death of handwriting should not be assumed. The dangers of email, the bashed-out "R U OK? I am gr8" ugliness of texting, the over-impulsive angry phone call — all these fade into white noise beside the elegant, deliberated simplicity of the handwritten note.

Crisp vellum stationery, the elegant flow of letters pouring across a page: these are the building blocks of our civilisation. Yes, we now have the printed word but do we want future civilisations to believe that ours was an age of bank statements and bureaucracy? Where are the love letters, the tellings-off from parent to errant teenager, the little *billet-doux* of correspondence that make the world go round? Stored on hard drives, listened to by bugging governments, deleted from voicemails? Handwritten notes are both personal and permanent; postcards survive to amuse well beyond the first 'Wish you were here' impulse, a love letter is worth a thousand texts.

Yet if the forces of modernity have their short-sighted way handwriting may no longer be an option. Schools no longer rate handwriting; homework is pecked out at home and taken in on memory sticks, greeting cards carry a message to suit every occasion. Unless we actively encourage our children to treat handwriting as a covetable skill, we face the danger of ham-fisted future generations, only able to touch-type, cut and paste. *See also Email*

HATS

Hats are compulsory at a diminishing number of social occasions. Women should wear a hat to Royal Ascot and smart race meetings; hats are traditional, but by no means compulsory, at weddings, and a matter of personal choice for christenings or funerals.

It is notoriously difficult to socially kiss while wearing a wide-brimmed hat. There is a knack to tilting the head at a suitable angle, but two ladies both in wide brimmed hats should avoid such an 'intimate' greeting.

Nowadays, gentlemen rarely wear hats except for morning dress, when grey felt top hats are *de rigueur*. They should be worn on the front of the head or carried under the arm, but should not be worn indoors or in the formal photographs. For the Royal Enclosure at Ascot, however, they are obligatory and must be worn at all times. It's also important to perfect 'doffing' a top hat — raising it above the head to greet guests with real panache.

Baseball caps are, primarily, a fashion for younger people. They should only be worn with casual clothes or for sport, and never back to front. *See also Morning Dress; Weddings*

HANGOVERS

'Always do sober what you said you'd do drunk. That will teach you to keep your mouth shut.'
ERNEST HEMINGWAY

Hangovers are generally self-inflicted, so you should approach the day after an evening's overindulgence with stoicism, and keep your misery to yourself.

Employers will not be impressed with employees who turn up for work feeling the after-effects of a night's boozing, especially if it interferes with standards of work. Make sure you arrive at work on time, keep your head down, drink gallons of water and black coffee, and don't tell everyone how many shots you enjoyed (or are regretting) the night before.

Classic hangover cures range from a fry-up, or bacon sandwich, to a Bloody Mary or other tried and tested 'hair of the dog' remedies. Of course, there is always the option of mitigating the effects of the alcohol: drink plenty of water, make sure you eat and call it a day before you're thrown out.

HEADPHONES

Tinny music emanating from headphones is an everyday hazard, especially on public transport. If you are using headphones, be aware that your music – distorted, percussive, maddening – may be painfully audible to your next door neighbour, and adjust the volume accordingly. But, for all their failings, headphones should always be used. It is the height of bad manners to inflict music, or a noisy DVD soundtrack, on other people in a confined public place.

HENLEY ROYAL REGATTA

This five-day regatta takes place in Henley-on-Thames at the beginning of July each year. Membership of the Stewards' Enclosure is restricted to those connected with rowing, for example people who have rowed at Henley in the past, and a dress code applies. Ladies wishing to enter the Stewards' Enclosure must ensure their hemline is below the knee and be aware that trousers are not permitted. Bare shoulders are fine and hat-wearing is not obligatory. Remember that high-heeled shoes will sink into the grassy banks. Men should wear lounge suits, rowing blazers or jackets and flannels, and a tie or cravat.

Behave appropriately in the Stewards' Enclosure. Do not move the deckchairs, use mobile phones or take drinks outside the roped-off bar areas. Children are not permitted.

No dress code applies in the Regatta Enclosure, although many people still choose to dress up. As with the Stewards' Enclosure, admission is by badge, but anyone can apply.

HICCUPS

Inherently comic (especially when tipsy), but deeply irritating, hiccups are involuntary and, arguably, should need no apology. But such an intrusive noise should definitely be acknowledged — "Excuse me, I seem to have got the hiccups" should cover it (no need to apologise every time!). If the attack goes on for a long time, and is becoming an annoying distraction, it might be best to withdraw to the bathroom, where you can experiment with a range of home

remedies (holding breath, drinking from wrong side of cup, doing handstands etc.) in private.

HONESTY

'It is always the best policy to speak the truth, unless of course you are an exceptionally good liar.'
JEROME K. JEROME

From a moral standpoint, honesty is always the best policy. Honesty is good; we live in a complicated world already, so why muddy the waters even more with murky lies? But as anyone who has ever blurted out an unacceptable truth knows, honesty can hurt. So is it better manners to be honest and hurt someone, or be dishonest and spare their feelings?

All too often honesty is a cloak for cruelty. As Disraeli quipped, 'Something unpleasant is coming when men are anxious to tell the truth'. Any sentence that starts with the phrase, "To be honest . . ." is going to be a sentence in which the speaker will hurt the listener's feelings or *amour propre*. Children are often cited as being admirably honest – "Out of the mouths of babes . . ." we coo indulgently. But this is because they are untrammelled by social niceties and able to express truths without fear of reprisal. If adults were this honest, we would all be miserable; marriages would founder over the smallest issues; politics would grind to a halt; industries would collapse. To be honest, honesty is now an elusive luxury: it is an upstanding moral value that should be revered and placed on a pedestal, but down here in real life, a little dishonesty is a far kinder thing.

HOSTS AND HOSTESSES

'When hospitality becomes an art it loses its very soul.'
MAX BEERBOHM

Hosting a social occasion is both a pleasure and a responsibility. For all but the most impromptu gathering, some careful planning will enable you to relax, and ensure that your guests enjoy a convivial atmosphere.

Check in advance that arrangements are clear. Your guests must know where you expect them to be, and when, including any directions and your telephone number in case of mishaps. Be clear about dress codes. If you would like guests to depart by a certain time, say so politely.

If you are serving food, recognise the limits of your culinary prowess and inclination. Your guests would rather enjoy your company over simple fare than attempt a fragmented conversation with you dashing frantically in and out of the kitchen. When hosting a larger gathering, be clear that your role is to oil the wheels of conversation, not to hold court with a favoured few. Don't let yourself be monopolised; brevity is essential. You may be the only person that some guests know, so be sure to circulate and make introductions where helpful. Be generous but not pushy with food and drink, and ensure that conversation is flowing.

As a guest, you should respond punctually to invitations; this will assist your host in making his or her plans. A prompt arrival, gracious demeanour, timely departure and a note of thanks will ensure that you appear on the guest list again, and a reciprocal invitation should follow where appropriate.
See also Dinner Parties; Parties

HOTELS

On arrival, ensure that you are happy with the room's location and standard: now is the time to negotiate improvements. A smile and civil behaviour should ensure that you receive the service you desire. Issues should be taken up with reception; only resort to speaking to the manager if you reach stalemate. If running late when checking out, a call to reception should secure an extra hour or two. Don't help yourself to bathrobes, fixtures and fittings.

On an extended hotel stay, ensure that the maid doesn't change linen every day – instructions are usually given in the bathroom. Leaving used towels on the floor or in the bath is an invitation to have fresh ones substituted.

In smarter hotels, tipping will be expected. Give a small gratuity (i.e. one or two pounds, euros, dollars, etc., as appropriate) to bellboys or porters per piece of luggage if they take your bags to your room. Doormen should be tipped upon checking out if they have helped with taxis or luggage. A banknote may be left in your room for housekeeping. Check whether a service charge is included in your room service bill. If not, add ten per cent at the end of your stay and ask that it be given to the appropriate staff members. *See also Bellboys; Tipping; Valet Parking*

HOUSEWARMINGS

When the stressful experience of moving home is over, and the dust has settled, what better way to relax and celebrate than with a housewarming party? Don't wait until your new home is a model of pristine, newly-decorated perfection; it's often a good idea to invite guests before you start the gutting and renovation process — it doesn't matter if they make a mess and spill red wine on your (soon to be discarded) carpets, and they'll enjoy hearing about your plans (which may never come to fruition). Housewarmings are an excellent way of meeting people who live nearby, and picking their brains about schools, shops, tradesmen, neighbours from hell, and so on. Old friends will enjoy being part of your new project.

If your good friend invites you to a housewarming it's a nice gesture (but not an obligation) to buy them something for their new home — glasses, ceramics, tableware or house plants are all good choices.

HUMOUR

'Humor is emotional chaos remembered in tranquillity.'
JAMES THURBER

Whether it's dealing with a train strike, a screaming infant or a senile parent, a sense of humour is one of life's essential tools. The most boring job can become tolerable if you can laugh with your colleagues about your boss's peculiarities. Even tragedies can become bearable if one can apply some gallows humour — "At least the house burning down means that we've finally got rid of Great-Aunt Enid's china dog collection". This is especially true if you can maintain a sense of humour about yourself. As one comedian said, 'The person who knows how to laugh at himself will never cease to be amused'.

The trouble is that imposing your own sense of humour on to others can be perilous — smirking at the vicar's adenoidal utterances during a funeral may be your way of coping with your upset, but it could well cause offence with the grieving family. Regaling a dinner party with a smutty story that you find utterly hilarious may not take into account others' more delicate sensibilities. Remember that if you are proud of your sense of humour, you need to be able to laugh at yourself: don't fall into the trap of thinking that everything is funny as long as it is happening to somebody else. It is one of life's awful truisms that they who boomingly insist that they have a terrific sense of humour are usually the least funny person you know . . . *See also Jokes; Teasing*

HUNGER

'No clock is more regular than the belly.'
FRANCOIS RABELAIS

Refrain from proclaiming "I'm starving" at the first twinge of hunger. You are not starving, and other people are unlikely to be interested in regular updates on your appetite. If hunger is making you tetchy, control your temper, and ensure that you eat sooner rather than later. Don't forget your table manners when you're hungry. There's no excuse for wolfing down your food without stopping for breath.

When you have finished your meal it is bad form to announce "I'm stuffed" or even "I'm full". If you do feel the need to give those around you a report a more polite way of phrasing it is simply: "I've had plenty".

HYGIENE, PERSONAL

This vexed question need never become an issue if you pay attention to a simple regular routine: daily showers/baths, frequent changes of clothing, use of deodorant, nail cleaning, and so on. If you're faced with a friend or colleague whose personal hygiene is questionable, try to address the issue directly (no anonymous 'gifts' of deodorant). Do it discreetly, and sympathetically, and make it clear that you're trying to help, not to embarrass.

HYPOCHONDRIA

Hypochondria is a widespread ailment of the modern age; everywhere we look there are chronic malingerers and delusion-sufferers who think that every spot is a rash, every sniffle is full-blown 'flu and every gasp is their last. It's also infectious; competitive hypochondria can be a terrifying epidemic unless controlled.

Hypochondria – with its anti-social symptoms of being work-shy, self-obsessed and, at worst, self-righteous about your needs as an invalid – accounts for millions of working hours being lost every year. But hypochondria is just so tempting. In this callous world we live in, it's no good expecting any sympathy for anything less than a full-blown medical condition so you might as well exaggerate just to get some attention. So go right ahead and moan to yourself that you're sure that cough is turning into pneumonia, just don't breathe a word to those around: they don't want your germs, imaginary or otherwise. *See also Illness, Discussing*

ILLNESS, DISCUSSING TO
INVITATIONS, WEDDING

ILLNESS, DISCUSSING

Everyone has days when they're oppressed by aches, pains and discomfort. But these are personal inconveniences, and should as far as possible be kept to yourself. Discussion of symptoms can all too often mutate into querulous complaints or, even more of a cardinal sin, over-explicit accounts of bodily functions. You should never be guilty of telling your listeners things they really don't want to know. If illness impairs your ability to function, be as honest about your problem as discretion permits. Soldiering on may seem brave, but is often simply stupid. *See also Bodily Functions*

INFIDELITY

'I would never be unfaithful to my wife for the simple reason that I love my house too much.'
BOB MONKHOUSE

Infidelity is like a hand grenade with the pin already taken out; you don't know when it will blow, there's a febrile excitement in the meantime, but blow you know it will. If you are determined to be unfaithful, then be a kind infidel, and try to be faithless without causing hurt (beyond your own eventual heartache), which means don't get caught. Be prepared to live like a spy, leading a double life, packed with credible lies and at the end of it, as end it will, be prepared to disguise any heartache and re-embrace your former life. Don't use close friends as alibis, or place them in compromising positions. It is quite unforgivable to test their loyalty in this way.

If you suspect a friend of having an affair – or if they have confided in you – restrain any impulse to interfere, or reveal all to the wronged partner. You dabble in the delicate architecture of a marriage at your peril, and may well find yourself blamed in years to come for wanton destruction.

INFORMALITY

The days when men referred to each other by their surnames, when office hierarchies were minutely calibrated by the use of the prefix 'Mr' or 'Miss' are long gone. Informality is the order of the day and first names are *de rigueur*; even in professional situations, when dealing with doctors, lawyers, policemen, bank managers, informality is being adopted. There is much to be applauded here – empty conventions are alienating and impede communication. But traditional fail-safes are very useful when you find it difficult to judge the social climate. If in doubt, opt for formality, and beware; older people may find the instant adoption of the first name disconcertingly overfamiliar. *See also First Names, Use of*

IN-LAWS

You know you're the luckiest person alive to have landed your perfect partner but when it comes to their relations, the laws of probability are not on your side. You've upset the balance of their family: at best you've swelled their ranks, further dividing the pot of love and attention, at worst you're the cuckoo in the family nest, stealing their beloved son/daughter/brother/sister. Even wonderful in-laws can create problems. If they're warm, uncritical, unfailingly supportive, always pleased to see you, dedicated and hands-on with their grandchildren and generous at Christmas-time, this will play merry hell with your relationship with your own less-than-perfect parents or siblings.

Treat a bad in-law as you would childhood chicken pox. You don't want it, you don't deserve it, you can't really do much to alleviate it, but it's a necessary evil and if you stay calm and are careful not to aggravate it, you'll come out barely scarred. Comfort yourself with the thought that your partner chose to leave the bosom of his/her family and create a new family with you – if the in-laws are truly toxic then your cleverest plan is to sit tight, behave immaculately and trust that there will be no doubt about which family is the better bet. As for perfect in-laws, don't boast about them to your own family (that way lies perdition) instead just secretly enjoy the fact that you've bucked the trend.

INSULTS, HOW TO RECEIVE

'It is only the vulgar who are always fancying themselves insulted. If a man treads on another's toe in good society, do you think it is taken as an insult?'
LADY HESTER STANHOPE

The challenge is to respond to insults in a way that maintains the moral high ground; you must never allow yourself to be dragged down to the insulter's level. Contain your anger;

don't snap back with an immediate, aggressive response —
you may say things you don't mean. Contemplate the insult
in tranquillity: consider the possibility that you may have
exaggerated or misinterpreted the insult; consult other
friends or witnesses and see what they think; confront the
(no doubt unpleasant) idea that there may be some truth in
what has been said. If you still feel the need to riposte, do so
in a calm and measured way — no emotion or intemperate
language. Keep your response pithy and concise, and don't
return the insult or you will rapidly become embroiled in
an ongoing conflict. Most important of all, rise above it.

INTERNET DATING

No longer the exclusive realm of oddballs and the downright
disturbed, internet dating gives the user the ability to pick
and choose without having to meet a multitude of no-
hopers. Choosing your date in much the same way as you
pick dishes from a menu lacks the finesse and subtlety of
traditional courtship, but it opens you up to a world of
possibility unavailable through conventional channels.

Honesty is always the best policy: being creative with
photographs or profiles will lead to eventual downfall when
you meet in the flesh. Use the best photograph you have:
if the picture isn't up to scratch, potential lovers won't even
bother reading the profile. It's a competitive world in
cyberspace, and to succeed you have to sell yourself. Steer
clear of clichés and innuendo, aim for wit without sarcasm,
and avoid excessive modesty as this will invariably backfire.

Keep initial approaches brief and light-hearted.
Officially it's rude to ignore overtures, so a brief response
is always appropriate. If you reach a stalemate with someone,
tell them rather than ignoring them. Not everyone will
abide by the rules of the game, though, so if you are ignored
by someone you've taken an interest in, give up graciously
after two messages are left unanswered. If you wish to turn
an online interest into reality, one of you must take the leap
of faith and suggest meeting in the flesh. Women should not
assume this is the man's responsibility, but issues of personal
safety when meeting a stranger should be considered.

INTERRUPTING

Breaking into other people's conversation, stopping
someone mid-flow, or finishing their sentences for them
will make you appear impatient and overbearing, and
should be avoided. If it is essential that you break into
a conversation – to relay some important news, or alert
people to the fact that dinner is served, for example –
establish eye contact with the person who is talking, and
then say "Please excuse me for interrupting, but ..."

INTERVIEWS

Notorious for striking fear into the hearts of even the most
self-confident, interviews are a genuine opportunity for
candidate and prospective employer to weigh each other
up. Immaculate presentation is essential, but gauge the

formality of the company first. Shake hands firmly, sit up straight, maintain eye contact. Judicious preparation is advisable, but remember that the interview is about *you* and not what you know about the organisation; select a few key facts to show you have done your research, and explain how your experience is relevant to the requirements of the job.

Don't be afraid to enthuse about your achievements, but be honest and never name-drop. Always ask questions; they provide a good opportunity for creating a more natural conversation and assessing the chemistry between you. Thank the interviewer warmly. Whatever the outcome, your response should be gracious. Never burn bridges.

INTRODUCTIONS

'Do you suppose I could buy back my introduction to you?'
GROUCHO MARX

If you are the link between people who have never met it is up to you to make the introductions. Remember the hierarchy: men should be introduced to women, juniors to elder people and higher ranks. Introduce individuals to the group first and then the group to the individual. For example, "Mary, this is Jim, Bob and Sue. Everyone, this is Mary." Unless the occasion is formal there's no need to mention surnames. If possible, offering a little information about each person as you introduce them ("Rupert and I were at school together") will help to break the ice.

When introduced, a friendly "Hello, good to meet you" is the standard response. *See also Forgetting Names; Handshakes*

INVITATIONS, OFFICIAL

Invitations to official functions give information about the nature of the function, the venue, the date, the time and, if desired, the time at which it is to end. For a daytime function (including a cocktail hour reception), the dress need only be specified if it is to be other than lounge suits; for an evening function, dress can be specified, for example, 'evening dress'.

An invitation to a pair of guests who are not husband and wife takes one of the following forms: brother and sister – 'Mr John Brown and Miss Elizabeth Brown'; mother and son – 'Mrs George Carruthers and Mr William Carruthers'; unmarried couple – 'Mr Paul Blaine and Miss Elsa Bond'. Invitations to adult offspring are sent separately from their parents'. Traditionally, only the wife's name appears on the envelope when an invitation is sent to a home address.

Guests should always use a reply card if one is sent out with the invitation. Alternatively, replies to invitations are sent on writing paper, showing the sender's address. They are written in the third person, for example:

Mr and Mrs William Brown thank the President and Council of the National Society of… for the kind invitation for Saturday, 12th February, which they accept with much pleasure (or: which they much regret being unable to accept).

INVITATIONS, PRIVATE

The formality of the invitation should accord with that of the occasion. More formal invitations are usually engraved or printed on good quality card, about 6 x 4½ inches

(15 x 11 cm) in size, and should include the name of both the host and hostess. The guest's name is handwritten on the top left-hand corner. Any specific dress code (e.g. 'black tie') and detail (e.g. 'Dancing 10 o'clock') may be stated.

Grown-up sons and daughters are usually sent separate invitations, even when they live at home. However, when their exact names, or their availability, are not known, it is permissible to add 'and Family' after their parents' names. Equally, the addition 'and Guest' or 'and Partner' may be added – the reply should name the 'Guest' or 'Partner'.

INVITATIONS, ROYAL

Royal invitations from the Sovereign are commands, so replies should be worded to reflect this and addressed to the member of the Royal Household who has issued the invitation. The reason for non-acceptance should always be stated – a prior engagement is not considered to be an adequate reason. An invitation to a garden party is accompanied by an admission card stating that an acknowledgement is not required unless a guest is unable to attend, in which case the admission card must be returned.

INVITATIONS, WEDDING

A traditional wedding invitation is made of cream or white heavy card measuring 6 x 8 inches (15.2 x 20.3 cm), folded in half, with the text (usually in black copperplate script) on the first page. The name of the guest is handwritten in ink in the top left-hand corner. On formal invitations, guests should be addressed by their full title, for example, 'Mr and Mrs James Jones' or 'Miss Eleanor Sweet'. For less formal invitations it is acceptable to use only first names.

The traditional format for a wedding invitation where both parents are married (though many families will not fit into this pattern) is as follows:

Mr and Mrs John Debrett request the pleasure of your company at the marriage of their daughter Charlotte to Mr Christopher Smith at The Church, Knightsbridge on Saturday 14th March 2015 at 3 o'clock and afterwards at The Swanky Hotel, London SW1

The RSVP address is placed in the bottom left hand corner of the invitation.

Sometimes, guests are invited to only the wedding reception. A note, giving a good reason, should be placed inside the envelope, for example:

Owing to the small size of St John's Church it is possible to ask only very few guests to the service. We hope you will forgive this invitation being to the reception only.

Replies should be handwritten, in the third person, on headed paper. The envelope is addressed to the hostess and the date is written at the bottom of the page. For example:

Mr and Mrs David Clegg thank Mr and Mrs John Debrett for the kind invitation to the marriage of their daughter, Charlotte, to Mr Christopher Smith at The Church, Knightsbridge, on Saturday 14th March 2015 at 3 o'clock and afterwards at The Swanky Hotel, and are delighted to accept (or: which they much regret being unable to accept).

JACKETS TO JOKES

JACKETS

A jacket worn with a shirt and tie and smart trousers is a standard interpretation of the stricter end of smart/casual, when an event does not require men to wear a suit. Equally, when a jacket is worn with smart jeans, a smart shirt but no tie, a man can be suitably dressed for the more relaxed end of the smart/casual spectrum.

There are many places in the country where it is still compulsory for a gentleman to wear a jacket. For example, the MCC Pavilion at Lord's, the Stewards' Enclosure at Henley and in all public areas at The Ritz in London.

JACUZZI

Cleanliness is crucial — shower first and ensure that your swimming gear is clean and chlorine-free. Generally, people prefer to enjoy a Jacuzzi in silence, so keep noise to a minimum. Don't splash or turn up the heat without fellow Jacuzzi users' permission.

JALAPEÑO PEPPERS

Jalapeño (pronounced *ha-la-pee-no*) peppers are a fiery addition to a dish. Cooks should be considerate towards those who will be eating what they prepare. Not everybody enjoys a mouth-scorching menu, and some people are actually allergic to chillis. Spice should be a flavour enhancer, so save very hot chilli dishes for tried and tested friends who enjoy a jalapeño challenge.

JARGON

Yes, we all have 'issues' with jargon; let's all be proactive about the way we interface, give it some face-time, run it up the flagpole and kick the tyres, then come up with a value-proposition that really shows we're tasked with thinking the unthinkable ... and so on.

The real problem with jargon is that it actually impedes communication. It's obfuscatory, rendering the simplest sentences opaque. It is frequently used to disguise ignorance, to wrong-foot colleagues and clients, to conceal ineptitude. It is anti-language, and anti-communication. If you are tempted to use jargon, think carefully about why you are doing so. Do you actually know what you are trying to say? Can you understand yourself? Why are you using inverted commas around certain phrases?

It is never a mistake to write, and speak, in plain, jargon-free English. You will be praised for the incisiveness of your thinking, and rewarded for your ability to communicate clearly. So why should you need to think outside the box?

JEALOUSY

'Jealousy is the greatest of all evils and the one which arouses least pity in the person who causes it.'
LA ROCHEFOUCAULD

Left untended, jealousy can be the canker at the heart of a perfectly good relationship. In some relationships, flirting with others and expressing admiration for someone else's beauty/charm/eligibility can pass without comment, relegated to the 'window-shopping only' category of behaviour. For other couples, such behaviour can breed real jealousy: but is it because one half is flirting too much or because the other half is over-reacting?

If your relationship is blighted by jealousy, try the 'other shoes' test — imagine how you would react to your partner if they were behaving in the same way as you do, and vice versa. The old-fashioned view was that a little jealousy was healthy to keep a relationship 'alive', but once unleashed, jealousy is tough to deal with. It is undignified to flash green eyes, and no one likes those conversations where one party is made to feel like a naughty school child and the other like a petulant brat. Much better, then, to head jealousy off at the pass.

If you see your partner flirting too much for your liking, neutralise it by joining in the conversation and endorsing the admiration, "Yes, don't you have amazing eyes?" which will bemuse all concerned. If you're the one flirting, and you see your partner starting to grimace, apply the 'other shoes' test; either extricate yourself gracefully and return to the nest or, if you still think they're over-reacting, just blow them an obvious kiss and carry on with your harmless badinage. Jealousy all too often stems from insecurity — better perhaps to ask yourself, or your jealous partner, exactly *why* you or they are feeling jealous . . .

JEANS

Before choosing to wear this wardrobe stalwart consider the occasion, the guests and the venue to help you decide if jeans

are appropriate. Let common sense prevail; don't wear jeans to a wedding, funeral, christening or other ceremony or important occasion. If you are mixing with the older generation denim may be frowned upon. If you are attending an evening do with a younger crowd you will probably be fine in smart jeans. But do remember that some bars and clubs, and nearly all members' clubs, have a 'no-denim' policy. Check ahead to avoid embarrassment. *See also Smart Casual*

JOKES

'A difference of taste in jokes is a great strain on the affections.'
T.S. ELIOT

Jokes are a serious business. Some of us mistakenly imagine that jokes make the world go round – that dinner parties wouldn't be the same without them, that our children must learn them from potty-training onwards, that the teller of a good joke will be a success at whatever they turn their hand to. There have been countless worldwide competitions, thousands of websites and even television documentaries, all to find the Best Joke Ever. Aliens landing in Britain would be bemused to find that we even have a day officially devoted to jokes, April Fool's Day. Jokes can also be an effective emotional release; post-disaster jokes are tasteless, tactless, cynical, exploitative ... and often horribly funny.

But the beauty of a joke is often lost on the beholder. Jokes can wither and die in the face of incomprehension or be artificially applauded in the name of 'politeness': a rich man's joke is always funny. Worse still, a joke can alienate or even cause offence, both in the joke-teller ("they just don't get my sense of humour in this country") or in the audience, ("actually, my wife is blonde and that's just rude").

As in all things, moderation is the key. Telling a joke can be a real conversation-stopper – if you're itching to relay the rib-tickler you heard earlier, appreciate that it will be disruptive, and tell it as quickly as possible before returning to real conversation. The second rule is to match your material to your audience: a filthy gag that had you and your friends weeping with laughter is probably not one to tell on your first day in the office. Great-Aunt Myrtle does not want to hear the latest blonde joke; that first date may not appreciate an erectile dysfunction side-splitter. Now, have you heard the one about the Englishman, the Irishman and the Scotsman ... ? *See also Humour; Teasing*

KEBABS TO KUMQUATS

KEBABS

Kebabs are small cubes of meat and vegetables threaded on to a skewer. Do not attempt to eat directly off the skewer: remove the meat before eating by holding the skewer in your left hand and using the tines of a fork to ease the meat, one piece at a time, on to your plate. Keep the tip of the skewer in contact with the plate for as long as possible, to avoid the meat flying off in surprising directions. Remove stubborn pieces by applying more pressure with your fork; never resort to using your fingers.

KEENNESS

'The world belongs to the enthusiast who keeps cool.'
WILLIAM MCFEE

Eager-beavers are the curse of the modern age. Gone are the mid-20th-century days when whippety keenness was prized and lauded; nowadays, it is seen as a short leap from keenness to weirdness, from zeal to fanaticism. Everybody despises the school swot, the teacher's pet, the pushy parent, the compulsive volunteer. The day of the tortoise has come; the hares are frankly embarrassing with their ungainly, breathless enthusiasm.

Of course, what we are actually advocating is the art of being a swan: all effortless elegance on the surface and furious paddling beneath. There is nothing more cool than the over-achiever who appears to have sauntered to their victor's throne, using only the force of their personality to propel them there. It's still the same old story of genius

KEENNESS

being, 'one per cent inspiration and ninety-nine per cent perspiration', identified by Thomas Edison in 1932 – just don't let that blood, sweat and tears actually show.

KERBSIDE, WALKING ON

A man should walk on the kerbside of the street. If, however, a woman naturally falls in step on the kerbside, then it would be clumsy for him to start dodging around her to try and walk on the outside. *See also Chivalry*

KILLJOYS

People who trail a bad atmosphere, casting an air of gloom and inhibition over other people's enjoyment are, quite literally, killjoys. It is alarmingly easy to become a killjoy: if you have had a bad day, or you are feeling tired and irritable, your mood can very easily infect those around you. If you are sour-faced and self-righteously intent on avoiding alcohol, and all around you are throwing caution to the wind, abstention can very quickly turn into disapproval. Strive at all times to be aware of the effect you are having on other people: if your influence is baleful, then bale out.

KILT ETIQUETTE

There are two rules when it comes to kilts: they should only be worn by those with a Scottish or Gaelic connection; and the correct attire must be worn to suit the occasion.

Formal kiltwear involves donning one's own tartan — modern, ancient or dress. Ensure that the length of the kilt is right: whilst the contemporary trend is towards the shorter kilt, which sits above the knee, traditional wearers insist that it should sit high on the waist — beneath the bottom rib, and rest between the top and middle of the kneecap. Accompaniments depend on the occasion. Daywear requires a plain tweed jacket, accompanied by plain sporran, shirt and tie, hose and brogues. The Prince Charlie or Kenmore doublet is appropriate for eveningwear. Marry this with a dress sporran, which is usually decorated with fur. For a more versatile and less formal look, don an Argyll outfit: worn with a standard white shirt and classic tie, this attire is suitable for Burns Suppers, ceilidhs and afternoon weddings.

When asked what you are wearing under your kilt, an enigmatic smile will suffice.

KINDNESS

'Three things in human life are important. The first is to be kind. The second is to be kind. The third is to be kind.'
HENRY JAMES

The foundation stone on which good manners rest, kindness is quite simply the ability to notice other people, recognise their needs or discomfort, and act upon that recognition. Kindness requires an ability to empathise with other people, and parents need to school their children in empathy — kindness and good manners will naturally follow.

KISSING, SOCIAL

Social kissing is a potential minefield and is usually dependent on situation, age, background, profession and your relationship. As a general rule, don't kiss people you don't know. Don't kiss colleagues. Do kiss close friends and dates. The key is to make your actions clear to avoid embarrassing confusion.

Usually it's right cheek first, but prepare to change direction at the last minute. Pull back decisively (but not abruptly) if you are just giving one kiss. Be cautious with those you are less familiar with — two might seem over the top. If confusion occurs over one-kiss-or-two, take charge and go in for a second. Humour is useful in deflecting embarrassment over the meet-in-the-middle mix-up.

Just holding cheek against cheek feels insincere, but there is a fine line between an acceptable peck and an overly affectionate smacker. Cheek skin must make brief, light contact; sound effects, air kissing and saliva traces are to be avoided at all cost. If you'd prefer to shake hands, be sure to hold yours out before any kissing manoeuvres begin but, if you're part of a group introduction, don't be the only non-kisser at the party. *See also Introductions*

KNOW-ALLS

We all know one of these — someone who believes that they possess a superior intellect and wealth of knowledge, and who shows a determination to demonstrate that superiority at every opportunity. In a world where knowledge is power,

the know-alls should be ruling the planet. Yet it seems to be one of those truisms, that the more a know-all someone is, the further they are from actually running things. After all, if they knew it all, they would know that it's the worst sort of rudeness to let everyone else hear about it.

We all love trivia, useless knowledge and the occasional weird feats of memory, but most of us — the know-somethings — have the sense to realise that it is not clever to trumpet such empty expertise. On the contrary, the get-aheads often seem unencumbered by sacks of facts or bushells of experience. While the know-alls are totting up the sum of their knowledge, the get-aheads are too busy getting ahead to sit and analyse whether they know quite a lot, enough or all of it.

If you are faced with a know-all, pity them for their lack of self-awareness, listen intently to their trumpetings for the odd interesting fact and never, ever disagree with them, for that way leads to perdition and the perfect excuse for the know-all to pummel you with further 'incontrovertible' facts. Then when you feel you've travelled as far as you can into the limitless vistas of the know-all's inner world, move on politely, leaving them, and their empty knowledge, behind you as you get on with real life.

KUMQUATS

Usually consumed raw, but occasionally cooked, kumquats are eaten whole including the skin. The top end may be cut off first.

LAUGHTER TO LYING

LAUGHTER

'There is nothing in which people more betray their character than in what they laugh at.'
JOHANN WOLFGANG VON GOETHE

It is somehow unsurprising that the old saying, 'Laughter is the best medicine' has now been put to the test. Studies have been conducted showing how people who can laugh at themselves and at life live longer and more happily. Laughter is aerobic and releases serotonin, which boosts your immunity, shoots pain-relieving endorphins around your bloodstream and even counters the effects of stress.

A little judgement should be exercised, however, before unleashing laughter indiscriminately. Laughing at a funeral is never acceptable, laughing at the wake afterwards can be a life-affirming release. Laughing at a child's entertaining first attempts to play their recorder will never endear you to their proud parents; laughing at their stories of the little one's potty-training escapades will make you popular. It's actually all about prepositions — laughing *with* but not *at*. Having a laugh with friends, family or loved-ones is what life is all about; laughing at someone else, or at someone else's expense will lead to trouble. Stay clear of such trouble by being a generous chuckler, momentarily checking at what or whom your laughter is directed and remembering that laughter can also be cruel.

As for how one laughs — just imagine that you're laughing into a mirror. If there's spittle on the glass or if you can see every twitch of your tonsils, then you question whether your laughter is charming or, frankly, frightening.

LEMONS

A wedge of lemon usually accompanies a fish or seafood dish. You can either squeeze the lemon with your fingers, or against the tines of a fork, which channels the juice. It is polite to cup your hand around the lemon while squeezing so you don't spray those around you, and squeeze the lemon low over your plate, not up high. If you are serving segments of lemon make sure you remove all visible pips.

LENDING

'Neither a borrower nor a lender be,
For loan oft loses both itself and friend'
WILLIAM SHAKESPEARE

Lending something to a friend should make us feel generous and bountiful, happy that we are able to help. In fact, what lending often does is taint that friendship and change its parameters. If a friend asks you to lend them something, they are effectively asking you how much you like and trust them. You are then placed in a difficult position. First, you secretly like them a little less for asking. Second, you can only say no for practical reasons (you physically can't afford to lend them money, for example); saying no for any other reasons effectively means that you don't trust them.

Before lending a valued possession, steel yourself to the likelihood that you may not get it back: and remember that it will seem rude and gauche if you ask for the return of your coat/money/book. If you must lend, be upfront and unemotional about your Terms and Conditions:

"Yes, you can take that coat, but I need it by the weekend in a good enough state to wear at a wedding".

So much better, however, to give, if you possibly can. Then it is within your control to limit or expand the gift, squash the sense of obligation and move on, quickly. After all, the balance of power in a relationship has shifted once you are asked if you can lend; why not use that power for good and come out of the situation with everyone happy? *See also Borrowing*

LETTER WRITING

'Sir, more than kisses, letters mingle souls; for, thus friends absent speak.'
JOHN DONNE

Always use quality stationery for correspondence, whether business or personal. Personal letters should be handwritten on white, ivory or cream paper, with a minimum weight of 100 gsm to avoid show-through. Use a lined undersheet to keep text straight, and use black or blue ink. A personal letterhead should include postal address, telephone number and email address, but never your name. If budget allows, have letterheads engraved. The envelope should match the writing paper and have a diamond flap. Always date personal correspondence. Don't frank pieces of personal correspondence — use a stamp.

Business letters must be typed, on A4 paper which includes the company logo, postal address, telephone number and email address. If any of this information does not appear on pre-printed business letters, be sure to add the pertinent contact details yourself. Type the recipient's name and address at the top left-hand side of the letter. The date goes beneath this, also on the left-hand side. Use 'Dear Sir/Madam' if you don't know the name of the recipient, although every effort should be made to discover their name. If you are familiar with the recipient, use their first name only, e.g. 'Dear David'. If in doubt, follow how they have styled themselves in previous correspondence. Otherwise, opt for formality.

Add a 'subject line' after the salutation – centre and embolden/underline it. This will be useful for sorting, prioritising and filing. Aim not to exceed one sheet of paper – it goes without saying that brevity and precision are vital attributes of business correspondence.

The sign-off depends on the salutation. As a broad rule, if you addressed the letter to 'Dear Mr Townsend' the sign off is 'Yours sincerely'. If addressed to 'Dear Sir/Madam', then 'Yours faithfully' is correct. *See also Envelopes*

LETTERS AFTER NAMES

Use letters after your name appropriately. For example, writing your university degree (BA Hons or BSc Hons) after your name when writing to friends looks pretentious. But including appropriate professional letters after your name on a business card makes good sense. No letters after the name should be added on invitations, but on formal lists and in professional correspondence they may be included.

There is an order of precedence for letters after names. The abbreviations 'Bt' or 'Bart' for a baronet, and 'Esq', if applicable, come first. These are followed by orders and decorations conferred by the Crown, which have their own order of precedence. Privy Counsellors and Appointments to The Queen are next, followed by Queen's Council (QC), Justice of the Peace (JP) and Deputy Lieutenant (DL). University degrees are written subsequently, followed by religious orders and medical qualifications. The next group of letters consists of: Fellowships of Learned Societies, Royal Academicians and Associates, Fellowships, memberships etc. of professional bodies and Writers to the Signet. MP (for Members of Parliament) is penultimate in the order of precedence, followed by letters denoting membership of one of the Armed Forces. *See also Debrett's 'Correct Form'*

LIFTS

It is important to remember that in lifts (like all enclosed public spaces) there is an invisible boundary around people. Generally, lifts command silence or hushed tones; don't shout or disturb your fellow travellers. Allow people out of the lift before you try to get in, and don't cram yourself in to crowded lifts.

If you are next to the control panel, you should take the responsibility for using it – politely select the correct floor for other people, hold the 'doors open' button if required or activate the 'doors close' button if everyone's in situ and ready to go. *See also Personal Space*

LISTENING

*'The reason we have two ears and only one mouth is that we may
listen the more and talk the less.'*
DIOGENES

Listening to a friend who is going through a divorce,
has suffered a bereavement, or lost their job, is the most
generous part of a friendship. It is generous because by
listening, and listening again, and listening some more, you
are stifling one of the keenest of human instincts, the need
to respond. This is crucial. Listening is not about waiting to
say your bit next. Listening is realising that nothing you can
possibly say at that moment could help as much as allowing
the other person to unburden themselves. You may or may
not be asked for an opinion at some point in the crisis but,
for now, listening is what you must do.

There is a skill in listening that goes beyond the ability to
remember later each tiny wail and moan for future reference
(although this is important). Stay focused, and nod and
shake your head at appropriate moments — never let your
eyes glaze over. Concentrate on what is being said and
maintain eye contact; listening while flicking through
a magazine or texting home to say you're going to be late,
is obviously not good enough. Beyond an immediate
crisis, listening attentively will serve you well in other fields.
Listening to the grapevine at work, listening when your child
actually confides something important to you, listening as
your aged parent casually mentions a trip to the doctor —
listening properly can often tell you far more than you
merely hear.

LOBSTER, EATING

A whole lobster in its shell will typically arrive at your table
already cut into two halves, allowing easy access to the flesh
for your knife and fork. It is also fine to use just your fork
while holding the shell steady with your hand. The big claws
usually come cracked but if not you will need to use special
lobster crackers. Once you've cracked the claws pull out the
meat with a fork. If you want to get meat out of the smaller
attachments use a lobster pick. Follow the same rules when
eating crab. If you are daunted by the extrication process,
opt for lobster thermidor; the white meat is extracted,
cooked and served in the shell. *See also Fish, Eating*

LOO

When nature calls, either slip away quietly or excuse yourself
from the group. Generally, loo is the preferred term,
'Ladies' or 'Gents' in public venues is also widely used.
'Toilet' is the internationally recognised word, but may
still raise an eyebrow in more class-conscious circles.
See also Bodily Functions; Urinals

LOUNGE SUITS

Lounge suits are normal business suits, worn for semi-
formal occasions with a shirt and tie. The equivalent for
women is a skirt or trouser suit, cocktail dress or sometimes
even an evening gown depending on the time of day and the
occasion. A hat is also appropriate at certain events for

women, so make sure you check the dress code. If 'lounge suits' are stipulated on an invitation, it is fine to ask your host if you need a little more clarification. *See also Smart Casual*

LOYAL TOASTS

Before the Loyal Toasts the toastmaster may ask for silence by saying 'Pray silence for…' You should get to your feet. The first and principal Loyal Toast is: 'The Queen'. The second Loyal Toast is occasionally given too. It follows straight afterwards and is usually limited to: 'The Prince Philip, Duke of Edinburgh, The Prince of Wales, and other members of the Royal Family.' *See also Formal Dinners*

LYING

'Any fool can tell the truth – the best liar is he who makes the smallest amount of lying go the longest way.'
SAMUEL BUTLER

Lying is an instinctive and unavoidable aspect of the human condition. We grow up to learn that we should not lie, that lying is a human vice and that telling lies will always get us into trouble in the end. Later on we also learn that lies are used on a multiplicity of occasions and come in all colours and all sizes: from irreproachable white to irredeemable black, via purple (embroidered truth), yellow (cowardly excuses) and grey (minor work-based deceptions). Ultimately, we realise that life is all the richer and more subtle for a few shimmering shades of truth.

How to be a good liar? In moral terms, lies that are told to be kind, or to spare hurt, will always triumph over lies that are told for their own sake, or to cover up wrongdoing. Don't overdo the fabrication: a life that gradually descends into a tissue of lies is a fragile thing – and others will distrust every single thing you say. In practical terms, a liar must avoid telltale signs like blushing, nervous giggling or rapid blinking and keep it simple. Stick to a bone of truth, merely fleshing it out with easily remembered exaggerations and logical extrapolations.

If you suspect that you are listening to someone else's pack of lies, there are three ways of dealing with it. You can ignore it: the lies are probably more to do with the insecurities and problems of the liar than they are to do with you. Or you can turn to forensic questioning – then sit back and watch them tie themselves in knots as they weave their tangled web of lies and struggle to remember each step. Or finally, if they are a loved one or a good friend, you can stop them in their tracks and save embarrassment with a well-timed and suitably mild remonstrance – "Come off it". But beware the rumbling of lies for they might herald the telling of uncomfortable truths and, as Samuel Johnson said, 'A man had rather have a hundred lies told of him, than one truth which he does not wish should be told'.

MA'AM TO MUSSELS, EATING

MA'AM

When you meet The Queen or other female member of the Royal Family for the first time you should address them as 'Your Majesty' or 'Your Royal Highness' respectively. From then on use 'Ma'am', which should rhyme with 'jam'.

In the Armed Forces junior officers address female superiors as 'Ma'am'. *See also Queen, HM The; Royal Family*

MAIDEN NAMES

It is traditional for a bride to adopt her new husband's surname upon marriage, but she is not legally required to do so. Many married women now choose to retain their maiden name, while others retain their maiden name at work, and use their new, married surname in non-professional situations. If a woman decides to retain her maiden name, she can adopt her husband's name at any time in the future without a deed poll.

A surname must be legally changed by deed poll if a couple choose to have a double-barrelled or hyphenated surname (combining both of their surnames) or if a bride wishes to use her maiden name as a middle name and adopt her husband's surname.

MAKING A PASS

This is a high-risk activity that often, though not always, involves lunging at an unwitting target. Consider it carefully when all your faculties are intact; never attempt it if you have overindulged, as you risk embarrassment for you both, particularly if the object of your desire is taken by surprise — he or she may consider your actions indelicate, or worse, disrespectful. Read the signals: if you suspect there is potential for romance, show your intentions with some relaxed but unmistakable flirtation. This gives your potential paramour the opportunity to consider the prospect and to make their feelings clear. If you are rebuffed, a regretful smile and a gracious withdrawal will leave the one that got away feeling flattered, and you with your dignity intact. *See also Seduction, Art of*

MASSAGE

Don't let anxiety over spa etiquette come between you and the serious business of relaxing. Massage is all about creating the optimum conditions for tuning out, so always assert your preferences on background music, clothing, pressure and chit-chat. This is not the time for empy politeness; enduring discomfort defeats the object. To prepare for your massage, you will usually be left to undress, lie down and cover up with a towel. Afterwards, you will probably be left alone again to regain consciousness. Don't feel obliged to leap up and grab your clothes — you will be prompted when your time is up. Some employers now offer a roving masseur or masseuse to keep the troops supple, relaxed and productive. When indulging in the workplace, some decorum is required. If no private space is available, keep your shirt on and sound effects to a minimum.

MATCHMAKING

'Courtship is to marriage, as a very witty prologue to a very dull play.'
WILLIAM CONGREVE

Matchmaking can be a deeply satisfying activity; a combination of puzzle (putting the pieces together to get the perfect combination) and good deed. Just as with any other aspect of courtship, there is a ritual and a rhythm to successful matchmaking. To start with, you must be a shameless networker, so that by sheer build-up of numbers, you can start to find prospective partners. Judge carefully whether you tell one, both or neither that they are being set up. Never make the mistake of matching like with like too minutely — if the chosen two are too perfectly matched and similar, there might be no friction, and therefore no spark. Resist the temptation to manage the match; once the couple have been introduced and the initial feedback has been parcelled back to the opposite party in judicial doses, the two should be left to get on with it. Meddling will only serve to heighten the dangerous artificiality of matchmaking.

If you yourself are being matchmade, don't trust your parents; it is highly unlikely that you and they are looking for the same things in your prospective partner. If you allow yourself to be matched, don't then get huffy when things don't work out. It's no good saying, "Why did you set me up with someone who didn't call?" when someone was good enough to look out for you in the first place. And if at first a match isn't successfully made, don't despair — there are hundreds of matchmaking services online, just waiting to find your perfect mate. *See also Blind Dates; Internet Dating*

MOBILE PHONES

'Telephone, n. An invention of the devil which abrogates some of the advantages of making a disagreeable person keep his distance.'
AMBROSE BIERCE

The ways in which this invaluable gadget can cause offence are legion, so always adhere to good mobile phone etiquette.

First and foremost, ensure that your mobile phone conversation is not disturbing other people. Don't use your phone in 'quiet zones' on trains, and even if you're not in a designated zone, be aware that your voice will distract a peaceful carriage of newspaper-reading commuters. Intimate conversations are never appropriate in front of other people – try and respect your own, and other people's, privacy. Don't carry on mobile phone calls while transacting other business – in banks, shops, on buses and so on – it is insulting not to give people who are serving you your full attention. Don't make calls to people from inappropriate venues; a call from a bathroom is deeply off-putting.

Switch off your phone, or turn it on to vibrate, when you are going into meetings, theatres, cinemas and so on. Choose your ringtone with care; zany, intrusive or comical ones can be deeply embarrassing in the wrong context, such as a business meeting.

Remember, above all, that you are not joined at the hip to this useful device. People in the flesh deserve more attention than a gadget, so wherever possible turn off your phone in social situations. Don't put your phone on the dining table, or glance at it longingly mid-conversation. If you are awaiting an important call when meeting someone socially,

explain at the outset that you will have to take the call, and apologise in advance. In social situations, excuse yourself and withdraw somewhere private to make or receive calls.
See also Quiet Zones; Text Messages; Voicemail

MONEY, DISCUSSING

At dinner parties across the country, civilised people are comparing their house prices, marvelling at the cost of each other's cars and revealing their bonuses and salaries. Where once an overdraft was a dirty little secret between us and our bank manager, now we discuss our debts shamelessly. We live in the Age of Information, with transparency as the new buzzword, right down to the see-through pay packets and credit cards colour-coded as to the bearer's wealth.

Somewhere along the way, we've forgotten the reasons why discussing money never used to be the done thing; so let's slow down for a minute and consider. We still live in a world of economical imbalance – there will always be Joneses to keep up with. So is it not a better, friendlier approach to keep such inequality as under wraps as possible? Bragging about one's bonus is a pathetic, and primitive, bid for supremacy: it just heightens the difference between your financial situation and that of the person you are talking to. Complaining about shortage of money all too soon tips into Micawber-like wheedling, guaranteed to make the people around you feel guilty. Money is the oil that greases the wheels of society but oil is filthy sticky stuff and we should clean our hands of it before coming out in polite company.

MOOD SWINGS

We all have good days and bad days, and moods can plunge or soar according to an array of factors, from blood sugar levels or hormonal overload to grey, oppressive skies. The important thing is to keep your fluctuating internal barometer strictly to yourself. No one wants to be subjected to your emotional highs and lows; your aim should be to project equanimity at all times.

If you do let your defences down and, Jekyll-like, unleash the snarling monster within, apologise (as soon as normality returns). Explain that you were temporarily deranged by hunger/insomnia/stress etc., and that your disconcerting behaviour was nothing personal. *See also Hunger*

MORNING DRESS

Morning dress (or 'formal day dress') is the traditional dress for weddings and formal daytime events in the presence of The Queen, such as Royal Ascot and Trooping the Colour.

The morning coat has curved front edges sloping back at the sides into long tails. It is single-breasted with one button, and usually has peaked lapels. Black or grey morning coats are nowadays considered equally acceptable.

Although grey is the traditional colour for a waistcoat under a black morning coat, patterned or coloured waistcoats are also acceptable. Brocade is a common choice, although silk might be more comfortable at a hot reception. Single-breasted waistcoats should be worn with the bottom button undone. If the waistcoat is double-breasted, all buttons should be fastened. Avoid backless waistcoats as you will not be able remove your morning coat.

Trousers should be grey with a grey morning coat, or grey and black striped (or grey houndstooth) with a black coat. One pleat down the centre of each leg is traditional and flattering for slim men. Flat fronted trousers are therefore more suited to heavier men.

Morning dress should be worn with a plain shirt (traditionally white with a stiff turned down detachable collar), although cream, pale blue or pink is equally acceptable. It should be double-cuffed, with appropriate cufflinks. The tie or cravat is traditionally of heavy woven silk. Black or silver is traditional, but non-garish pastels are frequently worn.

Formal black shoes should be laced-up and highly polished, worn with black socks. Grey felt hats are easier to come by than black silk ones. These are largely optional at weddings (except for the groom and his men) and should be carried rather than worn inside church. For the Royal Enclosure at Ascot they are obligatory and must be worn at all times. *See also Hats; Royal Ascot; Weddings, Attending*

MUSSELS, EATING

Use an empty mussel shell as a pincer to extract the other mussels from their shells. Using a fork is also perfectly acceptable. The sauce around the mussels can be mopped up with pieces of bread or with a spoon. Put all empty shells on the spare plate provided. *See also Fish, Eating*

NAILS TO NUDITY

NAILS

Ensure that nails are kept clean at all times. Do not cut or clean your nails in public. Don't let nails grow too long; this is especially important for men. Acrylic nails, nail art and nail jewellery can look tacky and are best avoided. The tendency to bite your nails should be resisted; it looks neurotic and bitten nails are unsightly.

NAME-DROPPING

The ever so casual, even whimsical, dropping of a name into a conversation is, more often than not, a crude attempt to gain social kudos from someone else's reputation. If you really feel that name-dropping is necessary, do it subtly; never mention a name out of context, and only refer to people you really do know. If you mention the names of people with whom you have only a fleeting, or nodding, acquaintance you will be seen, rightly, as a liar, and a delusional and needy stalker of celebrity.

NANNIES

The bad manners shown in front of nannies are astounding — an astonishing number of employers forget that their nanny is a person to whom they have entrusted their most precious possessions, their children, and treat her as if, at best, she were a deaf and dumb mute and, at worst, a skivvy. A good nanny is one who uncomplainingly looks after your children, deals with all things scatological, ferries them

about, plays with them with a patience that is remarkable and, above all, keeps them safe from harm. If treated right, your nanny can give you an unique 'third eye' insight into your children's lives, reporting on precious moments, hilarious conversations and, more seriously, those playground incidents of pain, bullying and humiliation that your child might be reluctant to reveal. Such guardians need to be prized and handled as carefully as the most delicate Limoges vase.

Treating nannies right involves being courteous, outlining clearly (from the outset) tasks, responsibilities and perks, trying to remember to couch your instructions as requests and bearing in mind that nannies have their own lives when it comes to days off and holiday requests. Such courtesy is, of course, a two-way street. Equally, you can expect a code of behaviour from the nanny: as a guest in your house (even if you're paying them to be there) you should expect a high standard of politeness, cleanliness, cheerfulness and willingness to help — especially if you have both agreed the clear parameters of the job at the beginning of the relationship. Nannies only get sulky if you start inventing new layers of responsibility and work for them.

Horror stories of anorexic, slovenly, sullen *au pairs* are matched only in their lurid detail by the accounts of parents trying to poach good nannies away. Tales of desperate mothers sleuthing round museums, spying on the nanny that is showing herself off best, shadowing her and then trying to woo her away into their employment are no exaggeration. The depths of behaviour to which some parents will stoop, faced with the prospect of being in sole charge of their pack of feral children unless they find a nanny, are legendary. Don't even consider joining their infamous ranks; such grubbiness may pay off in the short term, but your children will not thank you for the loss of dignity and decency that nanny-poaching entails ...

NAPKINS

Napkins (never 'serviettes') should always be provided and placed either on the side plate or in the centre of the setting, where the plate will go. They should be folded simply; avoid elaborate origami styles.

Before you start eating unfold your napkin and place it on your lap. Never tuck it into the top of your shirt. Dab the corners of your mouth with your napkin if necessary during your meal, do not make grand side-to-side wiping gestures. When you have finished eating place your napkin, unfolded, beside your plate. *See also Table Manners*

NEIGHBOURS

'There are two things we wish we could all live without: haemorrhoids and neighbours.'
SPIKE MILLIGAN

For all too many people, a neighbour is merely someone who has just run out of something, be it sugar or patience. Gone are the days when neighbours leaned up against each other's fences and chatted about the cricket while the wives

hung the washing out. In most cities, 'neighbour' is a dirty word ... they are all too often the ones who make the noise, grab the prime parking space, spill their bin-bags or fight with you over the party wall. Crimes committed on a domestic scale have become so mythical that 'Neighbours from Hell' programmes are now everyday fare on television and police have been brought in to address actual bodily violence between neighbours.

Don't feel the need to emulate such people, no matter how frustrating the late-night noise or the chip-fat smells. Avoid litigation too, if you can; once down the route of noise abatement orders and so on, you will always be nervous around your neighbours. If there are problems with the usual neighbour trigger points — noise, parking, rubbish disposal — try your best to negotiate the difficulties amicably and resist outright confrontation.

For most people, especially city-dwellers, neighbours need not just be a necessary evil. Make friends with your neighbours from the day you or they move in, and you will enjoy countless benefits. You can give them keys for when you get locked out, ask them to pop in and feed the cat if you're away, they'll know how to turn off the burglar alarm that mistakenly goes off when you've just left for your three-week holiday, they'll take delivery of parcels for you. If your children all make friends, you can offload yours onto them for hours at a time. Of course, these arrangements are reciprocal, and you must be prepared to do the same for them. But just by enlisting them as friends, no matter how artificially, you will have joined the local community.

NERVOUSNESS

'I only drink to steady my nerves. Sometimes I'm so steady I don't move for months.'
W.C. FIELDS

Nervousness is highly infectious. Try your best to hide the physical manifestations of nervousness – trembling hands, inappropriate giggling, jiggling feet, rapid speech – and you will find that being aware of, and controlling, the symptoms helps you to calm down. Use good manners as a convenient carapace that will ease you through the more challenging social situations – reverting to accepted social norms will disguise nervousness. If you notice that someone is feeling nervous, it goes without saying that you should deploy your best manners to put them at ease.

NOSE BLOWING

Sniffing loudly and repeatedly is inexcusable. Never be caught without a handkerchief or paper tissue. Most people have come to favour the latter, though carrying a clean, crisp cotton handkerchief is an outward sign of an organised life and will always impress. Before blowing your nose, excuse yourself from company wherever possible. In reality, privacy is rarely an option and discretion is sufficient. Hold one nostril closed and blow gently through the other. Not only is this technique quieter, but blowing hard through both nostrils can damage the ear. The process should be silent and brief. Fold your handkerchief and dispose of it quickly. Never use your hand. *See also Handkerchiefs; Sniffing*

NOSINESS

'I keep six honest serving-men, They taught me all I knew. Their names are What and Why and When And How and Where and Who.'
RUDYARD KIPLING

We'd all like to think of ourselves as having an enquiring mind, rigorously questioning the world around us and trying to add to the sum of our own human knowledge every day. Yet nobody likes to be known as a nosy person, a prying old busybody. There is clearly a fine line between acceptable curiosity and unacceptable nosiness. Are we being nosy if our enquiries take us beyond the need-to-know?

The answer lies within ourselves. If we are sleuthing for prurient, non-educational reasons, then we're being nosy; if we are poking about because a situation might affect our lives/decisions/dinner plans, then fair enough. In our dealings with our friends, a natural desire to be a confidante and offer well-informed comfort/advice can sometimes tip over into a voyeuristic salivation over gory details. One acid test could be that if you're mentally marking down the salient points in order to pass them on to another friend then, yes, you're being nosy.

NUDITY

'I don't have an Achilles heel, I have an Achilles body.'
WOODY ALLEN

Some people would fervently claim that nudity is marvellous; it's liberating, invigorating, just what nature intended. Others argue that nudity is disgusting: wobbly, hairy, mottled, chilly – and advocated precisely by the people who should, frankly, cover up. Which view do you hold? The sight of untrammelled flesh will always provoke strong reactions, and nudity, whether on a public beach or in a private garden overlooked by other houses, is no exception.

Just as one covers up in Muslim countries, there is an element of 'when in Rome' about accepting nudity on beaches in parts of Europe; but consider whether your friends or family will ever forgive you if you follow (lack of) suit. Even in the most naturist of environments, do imagine the feelings of others being faced with your nudity. Assess the climate in communal changing rooms: if nudity is prevalent, then it is wise to bare all – you don't want to look ridiculously inhibited and body-shy. Don't strut your stuff if modesty prevails.

As for nudity inside the house, basic rules of family decency apply: you wouldn't cut your toenails or floss your teeth in front of anyone except a family member, so follow the same guidelines for nudity. Greeting the nanny or the postman in your altogether will only embarrass all concerned. And if you're prone to walking around without your clothes on, just take pity on the scorching perma-shame of teenagers.

OFFICE PARTIES TO **OYSTERS**

OFFICE PARTIES

Behind the gloss of festive celebrations and the camaraderie of leaving do's is the reality that you are socialising with colleagues under the watchful eye of those higher up the food chain. Be smart and social, but know when to draw the line. Circulate and socialise, but keep it upbeat and general. Ask about families, children and holidays. Don't gossip, spread rumours or confess your sins. Steer clear of mistletoe and dirty dancing, and keep goodnight kisses innocent.

Remember the basics: avoid shots, eat well, alternate drinks with water. Have fun and a few glasses, but don't be the casualty everyone is talking about (and sniggering at) the next day. If things start feeling dangerous, call it a night. The day after still counts too. Crawling in hungover and late (or worse, pulling a sickie) is unforgivably unprofessional.

OFFICE POLITICS

Few deskbound workers are spared the tribulations of office politics. Enforced proximity for eight or more hours a day is a breeding ground for gossip, rivalry, friendship and romance; some thrive on the drama, while many simply endure it. It is inevitable that you will become involved in the politics of your office to a greater or lesser extent, but only participate in a way that you can reconcile with your conscience. Be prepared to take the consequences of your actions if you indulge in political machinations. When you encounter challenging or delicate situations with colleagues, handle them as sensitively as possible, the basic rules of politeness should always be followed: avoid confrontation unless you find turbulence exhilarating or your workplace demands it. Idle gossip can be very damaging, so abstain wherever possible. However petty, juvenile or ruthless your colleagues may seem, remind yourself that they are human beings with lives outside the office. Treat all colleagues with courtesy, irrespective of hierarchy. *See also Business Trips*

OFFICE ROMANCE

'He and I had an office so tiny that an inch smaller and it would have been adultery.'
DOROTHY PARKER

The camaraderie of the workplace can often overflow into romance, but you should think carefully before embarking on a relationship with a colleague. Be guided by common sense and consider potential conflicts of interest; it's also worth checking whether your employer has a policy on such matters. However professional you are, others might be quick to suggest that your judgement is clouded. A liaison between boss and subordinate is particularly problematic and may require one of you to consider your options.

If it's early days and you're not sure whether your romance has staying power, be as discreet as possible and keep it between yourselves. If you become an established couple, it is worth considering whether to spill the beans, with a view to controlling the spread of the news rather than relying on the office grapevine. Never flaunt your romance in front of colleagues: displays of intimacy will undermine your professionalism and make others uncomfortable. You will gain the respect of others by showing restraint. With careful handling and favourable circumstances, romance can blossom. However, if you find that mixing business with pleasure is affecting your work or your relationship adversely, assess your priorities and act decisively.

OLD PEOPLE, RESPECT FOR

'And in the end, it's not the years in your life that count. It's the life in your years.'
ABRAHAM LINCOLN

Our perception of what constitutes 'elderly' is changing. Older people are staying healthier for longer and pride themselves on retaining their youth, so the business of respecting our elders can be tricky. In times past, the elderly occupied an elevated position in society and were treated deferentially, but this can now seem disproportionate or even patronising. However, some people will expect this and you must trust your judgement.

In practical matters, always be patient. When travelling on public transport, it is perfectly correct to offer your seat to a person who appears to need it more than you, but don't be offended if they decline and don't let this put you off in the future. If you are in conversation with someone who is hard of hearing, avoid shouting or speaking more slowly than usual. Speak audibly and articulately, and be guided by them. Be patient: older people are likely to eat more slowly, and walk more slowly than their younger companions.

If you are an older person, show reciprocal patience and respect for your juniors. A polite response will go a long way. Reacting badly to what you consider to be an over-the-top demonstration of respect will embarrass and discourage younger people from acting kindly in the future.

ONLINE MANNERS

The online universe is about communication: people meet each other online, tell each other jokes and secrets, argue, discuss. But just because you are apparently interfacing with a machine does not mean that manners should be forgotten. Make it a general rule that you will never say anything online that you wouldn't be able to actually articulate directly, face-to-face. The internet is, after all, there to facilitate communication, not to preside over its general breakdown.

Do not use the technology as a shield, masking your true feelings and personality. So always write polite emails, and never send messages (on social networking sites, chatrooms, SMS etc.) that contain intemperate language or sentiments that you would never normally express in your everyday life. Don't be an online bitch: skulking behind the computer screen and dishing out poison. Don't be an online bully: threatening and haranguing people you can't see, who can't fight back. Don't be an online bore: blogs that enumerate the minutiae of your day, likes, dislikes etc. in tedious detail exercise a horrible fascination, but won't make you popular.

Always remember that going online is a way of enhancing your life, not a substitute for living. *See also Social Networking*

OSTENTATION

Ostentation would seem to be the guiding principle of
the modern world — the bigger the bank balance, the more
flamboyant the toys, the showier the bling, the more column
inches. There are whole industries of publicists, PR execs,
agents, managers and spokespeople who live to show off;
whole rafts of the media whose sole aim in life is to report
such ostentation; and whole sections of society who enjoy
nothing more than reading all about the yachts, the parties,
the million-dollar-necklaces.

But if you haven't put in the grim and grimy effort of
working towards success then you haven't earned the right
to be irreproachably ostentatious. Ostentation without a
track record of achievement is just vulgarity. We've wandered
a long way from the unassuming, 'less is more' discretion
of the past, but do we not secretly still admire the sheer class
of those powerhouses of industry, finance or the media who
remain more private than public, more whispered-about
than talking-out? Yes . . . but don't go too far: flaunting
riches and success is one thing, being ostentatiously low-key
and scruffy when everyone knows you're worth millions is
just irritating for those of us who'd love to prove how much
fun we'd have with the money. *See also Understatement*

OVERFAMILIARITY

It's the left hand sneaking round the back of your elbow as
you shake hands. It's the sly nod and the conspiratorial wink
in conversation with others when you've got no idea why you

are suddenly linked. It's the 'darling, sweetie, love' from someone whose name you are still struggling to remember. It's the horror of meeting someone at a dinner party who within seconds is confessing their inability to hold on to a boyfriend. Common to all is the hair-raising chill and miasma of dread that heralds the overfamiliar.

Taking intimacy for granted is a sure-fire way to estrange; slapping your new boss on the back on your first day has you destined for the post-room. If familiarity breeds contempt, overfamiliarity propagates pure bile. Overfamiliarity often masks, at best, offputting insecurities and, far worse, a real idleness. People who think that they can go straight to Intimacy without passing Go and without slogging through all the Old Kent Roads of developing a relationship do not deserve to have a Monopoly on your friendship. After all, true friendship is not a game. *See also Friendship*

OVER-REACTION

It is no longer enough to win a prize in a competition and say, "Oh jolly good. Thanks awfully"; we must scream and yell and clutch our faces in dumbfounded disbelief. It no longer carries any weight when we tut and shake our heads when queue-barged at the supermarket; we must shout and stamp. Children are no longer satisfied with a pat on the head; they must be congratulated at every turn, praised effusively for merely trying, let alone winning, and generally made to feel like gods and goddesses. We live in an age of burgeoning over-reaction and it's getting exhausting.

Where do we go for our reactions to real achievement, real despair, real anger? Strangely, back round the circle to the smallest reaction of all: silence. Far more affecting than the wailing and weeping at Princess Diana's death was the silence with which the crowds greeted her funeral cortège. When giving a child a present, far more touching than an overblown yell of "Awesome!" is seeing the look of speechless wonder that crosses their face. You know you have fed a roomful of people well when they're too busy eating to remember fulsome compliments and empty flattery.

Of course, over-reaction is often a mask for unworthy real feelings – the exaggerated mugging smiles of the passed-over Oscar nominee, the "Wow! Isn't it gorgeous!" when your child hands you a misshapen excuse for a clay pot – and it is surely kinder to feign an exaggeratedly polite reaction than show the real negative one? The trouble is that the currency of reaction has been terminally devalued: the more showy the fake reaction is, the more obviously counterfeit it is. React in a measured way. Avoid the empty posturing and bring back the subtler measures. Over-reaction is over.

OYSTERS

Oysters are served in their shell. They should come already shucked (i.e. detached) but use your fork to prise the flesh from the shell if any sticks. Squeeze lemon juice over them then pick up the shell, bring it to your lips and tilt it to slide the oyster into your mouth. If you prefer, spear the oyster with a fork. Don't chew it; swallow it whole. *See also Fish, Eating*

PARTIES TO PUNCTUATION

PARTIES

'I don't know a lot about politics, but I can recognise a good party man when I see one.'
MAE WEST

The party scene is packed with countless variables. No two gatherings are ever the same, and even with an identical venue, refreshment and music, no party can ever be recreated. Atmosphere is an elusive commodity, and it falls on the shoulders of the host to create the right conditions for *bonhomie* to flourish.

As a host, it is your obligation to make your guests comfortable. This means, first and foremost, ensuring that they have plenty to eat and drink, and that everyone is socialising. You should introduce your friends to each other, and ensure that there are no wallflowers. But do not take this too far; interrupting animated conversations and dragging people across the room because there is 'someone they must meet' is very bad manners. If there are spills or breakages, clear up quickly and efficiently, and do not make a fuss. As a host, it is your duty to stay to the bitter end – even if a party is evidently flagging, you should not leave your guests simply to 'get on with it'.

If you are a guest, you should always respond to an invitation punctually and if you accept, attend. If possible, allow yourself half an hour more than you think you need to get ready; you will create the right impression and arrive in a better frame of mind. Arrive in good time but avoid being early; your host may be thrown off course by having to entertain whilst making last-minute preparations. However stressful your day has been, leave any anxiety at the door. You are here to enjoy yourself and to help others do the same. A drink will help you unwind, but be careful not to overindulge. This also applies to food; avoid stationing yourself by the buffet all evening, and never pursue a tray of canapés through a crowded room. When engaged in one-on-one conversation, give the other person your full attention and be as lively and stimulating as you can. Never look over his or her shoulder for an escape route or a better offer. It is worth having one or two credible techniques up your sleeve to detach yourself from a conversation that is going nowhere. Always thank your host warmly and follow up with a note of thanks. *See also Buffets; Canapés; Conversation; Hosts and Hostesses*

PEAS

Avoid turning over your fork and using it as a scoop; instead, squash the peas on to the back of the fork. Utilise any aids on your plate, such as mashed potato. Scoop with an upturned fork in more casual or solitary situations.

PERFUME

Exercise moderation when it comes to perfume; don't overpower those around you. Be particularly aware of overuse in confined spaces such as cars or aeroplanes. Wear a delicate fragrance for daytime and reserve stronger scents for the evening.

PERSONAL SPACE

It is an undeniable fact that some people always stand too close. Even on crowded public transport, there is inescapably close and threateningly close. When someone steps over that invisible line, when you start to feel troubled, you want to step backwards away from the space-invader, and you focus less on what they are saying than on how close they are to you. The trick here is not to back away but to somehow create a whole new space: turn to wave hello to someone passing, turn away to get something out of a bag, at the same time subtly putting some clear water between you and the invader. If you suspect that you are the person that unknowingly is the space-invader, then apply the following test: if you can feel the warmth of their anxious breath upon your face, then you're standing too close.

We are becoming increasingly unused to sharing our personal space. Communal living outside the family unit is at an all-time low – so that people don't even get to practise their space-sharing skills on flatmates. We are so insulated from the outside world by our MP3 players, mobile phones and fear of catching an aggressive stranger's eye on the street that it is rare for anyone under the age of 40 to even acknowledge their physical environment. Social networking sites remove us one step further from actually having to interact with people; but even that virtual personal space is being increasingly invaded – by Big Brother companies who dig out every personal detail they can to establish our voting preferences, our retail profile, our ability to finance mortgage payments. Employers now have a propensity to invade would-be employees' personal space by checking out their social networking site ... unearthing every embarrassing picture, every drunken posting, which then prejudices their hiring decision. Even online, guard your privacy in the same way that you would in 'real life': apply the same judgements to making friends, or even 'catching someone's eye' as you would in the outside world.

We need to preserve our personal space, both in the real world and the virtual one, but not at the expense of any intimacy at all. So get out there and start interacting with people — just don't stand too close. *See also Lifts*

PETS

If you are an animal-owner you are more than likely an animal-lover, happy to share a bed with your cat, thrilled by the tuneful twittering of your budgerigar, undeterred by your dog's sloppy chops. But you must remember, above all, that not everybody shares your enthusiasm. Check first, and if your visitors are hesitant or confess to an allergy to cat hair, don't inflict your animals upon them. Insouciantly exclaiming "she really likes you" as your visitor flinches from the insistent kneading of a sharp-clawed cat, simply won't do. If you have guests, keep pets out of their bedrooms, unless enthusiastically requested to do otherwise. Don't anthropomorphise your pets in public: you may think of them as furry near-humans, but cloying 'conversations', complete with baby voices and sugary endearments, will embarrass your visitors. *See also Dogs*

PIPS AND STONES

Pips and stones (cherry, olive etc.) should be discreetly
spat into a cupped left hand and deposited on the side
of the plate or discarded.

PIZZA

Pizza can be eaten with your fingers or a knife and fork,
depending on the formality of the situation. When eating
with your fingers, bend the slice lengthways and take bites
from the pointy end, taking care not to lose the topping.
Beware unsightly strings of melted cheese. Using a knife
and fork is a better idea if you're in a restaurant.

PLASTIC SURGERY

*'I was going to have cosmetic surgery until I noticed that the doctor's
office was full of portraits by Picasso.'*
RITA RUDNER

Walking into a fancy cocktail party of people over 40
these days can often be reminiscent of a trip to Madame
Tussaud's; on all sides is perfection but some are more
glassily perfect than others – a slight sheen to the features,
a waxy stillness to the forehead, a raise of the eyebrow that has
been preserved as if in aspic, a suspiciously bee-stung lip,
a bosom that looks held up by a force that supersedes gravity.

Whether you agree or disagree with the impulse to deploy
the cosmetic surgeon's art to hold back nature's tide, the
people who have had plastic surgery have made their choice

already and it would be rude to mock them for it. Indeed, people who have turned to the pain and expense of surgery to make themselves feel better about their physical appearance deserve exceptionally careful handling. So flatter to deceive and be subtle – don't admire the cut of the surgeon's knife, merely tell them how great they look. After all, many people are manifestly unwilling to admit to the fact that they've had surgery at all; if they choose to be secretive, do not challenge them.

If you have had plastic surgery yourself then don't imagine that just because it's cosmetic means that it is any more discussable than any other surgery. You wouldn't talk about the details of your gallbladder removal at a cocktail party, so nor should you wax lyrical about the faulty silicone implants you've just had removed in favour of some far superior saline ones. This is too much information; keep it between yourself and your surgeon.

POLITENESS

It is an incontrovertible fact that you can be impeccably punctilious about all the trappings of manners – opening doors, pulling out chairs, walking on the kerbside edge of pavements etc. – but still be appallingly rude. The call centre employee has been well-coached in the etiquette of the cold call or the politest way of handling complaints – yet, with every meaninglessly courteous and obfuscating syllable that falls from their lips, we are driven to incontinent rage. Politeness is not a failsafe measure of manners.

Manners are valuable in this world for the simple reason that well-mannered people know how to set others around at their ease, know how to make the world feel a more civilised, friendly and calm place, and like to put others' comfort ahead of their own. If politeness demands that dinner parties are seated boy-girl, boy-girl, good manners demands that when your guests take it into their heads to sit randomly, you just smilingly go with the flow. If being polite and opening a door for someone means that you have to wrestle your way past them in the first place, almost knocking them flying, then why not stand back, relax and with good manners acknowledge their own kindness in holding the door open for you.

Yet don't cast politeness out entirely — it is a good plank in the raft of manners and should be respected as part of the social contract we should all tacitly enter into to make our world more harmonious. The trouble is, politeness is already seen as old-fashioned; we seem to like our artists, our celebrities, our politicians and lions of industry to be mad, bad and dangerous to know, unfettered by the bourgeois standards of morality and politeness. It's not too late — even in the artificial world of reality TV, we've seen the occasional polite, quiet entrant triumph over their louder, brasher competitors. But we need to preserve politeness as the vital ingredient in the cocktail of manners that makes our world a better place; somewhere where basic survival is finessed into a more subtle pleasure. So bring back the doffing of hats, bring back the polite boardroom, let's have unisex chivalry. *See also Chivalry*

POLITICAL CORRECTNESS

'I am free of all prejudice. I hate everyone equally.'
W.C. FIELDS

Political correctness may have had its roots in wanting to minimise offence given in our language or attitudes to racial, cultural or other 'identity' groups, but it is now a pejorative term: a pure example of how a good thought can go terribly wrong. Nowadays, every level of madness is invoked in the name of political correctness. Policemen have been told to talk about people who have killed themselves as 'victims of self-harm' in case the word 'suicide' offends. Short people are 'vertically challenged', the unemployed are 'un-waged', and so on. One could get depressed that, with the real problems facing our world, anyone could get distracted by such nonsense. Or one could take a more trenchant view. PC is the policeman of society – better perhaps, to nod politely at it as you go past and just try never to get involved in a situation where it will be called upon to stand in judgement.

POLITICS, DISCUSSING

The world would be a very bland place if no one ever argued about politics. However, emotions frequently run high around political issues, and you should therefore treat this issue with care and respect.

If you're in an environment where a stand-up, passionate political row is not desirable (an office, a dinner party where you're being introduced to your fiancé(e)'s parents etc.), then it is probably a good idea to lay off politics altogether, or at least gauge the prevailing political climate – in these circumstances, a heartfelt consensus is bonding, dissent is likely to be damaging.

In a more knockabout environment, there is no reason not to join the fray. Just be sure that you know what you're talking about and have the facts straight before you lay into anyone. Your arguments will be much more persuasive if you keep calm, listen to other people and treat their views with respect. *See also Arguments*

PORT ETIQUETTE

Port is traditionally served after pudding with the coffee or cheese course. If you are at an informal dinner party or a restaurant no ritual will be involved, but take more care at a formal dinner when you should not take a sip before the Loyal Toast. A port decanter will be placed on the table so that you can help yourself and then pass it on. Always pass the port to the left. If the port passes you by without your glass being filled don't ask for the port and make it change direction. Just send your empty glass after the port decanter and ask for it to be filled. *See also Digestifs; Formal Dinners*

POSTCARDS

When picture-postcards were first sent out in the 19th century they were the Victorian equivalent of today's text message – pithy, informal, to the point. There is little

etiquette surrounding postcards: you do not normally
have to start them with a salutation (you can go straight into
the message), and you do not need to employ any particular
sign-off. They form a verbal snapshot: a message from
a particular place (most typically a holiday location); or
simply a reminder that you are thinking of a person. If
possible, eschew the obvious postcard clichés, and inject
your postcard with personality – a humorous observation
or a personal reference that proves you're actually thinking
of the recipient, not fulfilling an empty obligation. In the
modern age of email and text messages, a snail-mail
postcard is a thoughtful gesture.

POSTPONING

Postponing a rendezvous, date or other social event is
unavoidable from time to time, and to postpone politely
you must be prompt. Make contact with the other party as
soon as you know that you're unable to make the appointed
date. If you leave your postponement to the eleventh hour
– unless you have a very good reason – you will demonstrate
a lack of respect for the person you're meeting. Do not
become a serial postponer; it is remarkably easy to acquire
a reputation in such matters, and people will stop taking
future arrangements seriously.

Make contact by telephone if possible. Taking the time
to ring reassures others that you value their time and intend
to honour future commitments. An email or text message
is acceptable only if you are unable to get through by phone.

Choose your wording carefully to avoid appearing offhand. Explain your reasons as honestly as possible. If a clash arises, as a general rule you should honour the first commitment you made, but use your judgement; in exceptional circumstances, a friend will understand if you explain the pressing nature of the alternative. Try and reschedule your engagement as soon as possible. *See also Cancelling*

PRAWNS

Always confront a prawn with confidence, and don't be afraid to get your fingers dirty. If your prawn arrives intact, begin by the removing head and tail; do this by giving each end a sharp tug. Peel off the shell, starting from the underside where the legs meet the body. If your prawn is uncooperative, discreetly bend it against its natural curve to loosen the shell. Finally, remove the black thread from along the back before devouring the flesh. To eat a prawn served headless but with its tail attached, use the latter as a handle and discard after eating the flesh. *See also Fish, Eating*

PREGNANCY

'I positively think that ladies who are always enceinte quite disgusting; it is more like a rabbit or guinea-pig than anything else and really it is not very nice.'
QUEEN VICTORIA

In the early and late days of pregnancy it is easy to imagine that you deserve to have better manners shown to you than

your fellow unpregnant woman or man. Early on, you may be feeling tired and nauseous; in the last weeks, you're sharing an already cramped body with a lodger who keeps you awake at night, and renders you unable to walk without looking like a stately barge. In both cases, you could argue, you are entitled to better treatment from those around you — and few would disagree. But you should resist the megalomania of pregnancy; it may feel earth-shattering, but women have been doing it — sometimes with no fuss at all — for millennia.

Pregnant women should be given the seat on the tube, should be asked to sit down and take delivery of cups of decaffeinated tea wherever possible and should be shown every possible consideration but, if you are pregnant yourself, remember to react as if you are being shown beautiful manners, not as if it is your right and expectation to be fussed-over and pampered.

Of course, the minefield of establishing whether someone is pregnant often means that such kid-glove treatment isn't proffered. Offer your seat on the train to a portly woman at your peril: the chances are you'll offend her as much as you wanted to look out for her. When someone says that they are not drinking, never say, "Oh right, not in your condition," unless you have a disregard for your own personal safety. Never assume that someone is pregnant until they either tell you or place their hand wearily into the small of their back in the international gesture for "Yes, it's okay, I am pregnant". Then, and only then can you roll out the programme for treating a pregnant woman politely.

PREGNANT PAUSES

Never be fooled into thinking that, in conversational terms, silence is simply a point when no one is talking. A pause in conversation can speak volumes, and should be used consciously and discerningly. If someone asks you what you think of their new décor, and you pause for more than a beat or two, before blandly answering "Very nice", then you have used a pregnant pause to indicate, at the very least, ambivalence about the colour scheme. Pregnant pauses can also be used to create drama and tension in your discourse: your audience is transfixed as they wait for your next utterance, and expectations are high. If you follow this suspense-laden pause with a humorous or bathetic remark you will be applauded for your comic timing.

PRESENTS

A time-honoured way of showing affection, gratitude or esteem, or marking rites of passage, such as birth or marriage, the giving and receiving of presents is one of life's greatest pleasures. Presents should always be given in good faith and with the sole intention of delighting the recipient. A thoughtful present should be appreciated regardless of cost. The time you have taken to select it will be apparent in your choice. However, if you do not know your recipient well, certain presents have enduring appeal and will always be appreciated.

Generally speaking, the present should be appropriate to the depth of your acquaintance and to the reason behind the gesture. If possible, do some research to avoid making a basic error — the bottle of whisky to the teetotaller, or the chocolates to the dieter. Beware: present-giving is not a competition, and there is no need to go over the top. A competitive spirit undermines the action and a disproportionate show of wealth is likely to embarrass the recipient, and create a sense of reciprocal obligation.

When selecting presents for those close to you, think carefully about their tastes, hobbies, passions. Never fall into the trap of buying a present that you really want for yourself, and that you fully intend to use, borrow or adopt. Remember what you have given in the past. A repeat present suggests that you take the whole business lightly, so keep a list if your memory is poor. Try not to agonise over choice and never try to match the anticipated value of a reciprocal present. Giving and receiving are entirely separate activities, and this is not the time to weigh up the *quid pro quo*. To ensure that giving is truly better than being on the receiving end, take the time to plan. A last-minute trip to the shops will leave you frazzled and spoil the experience. A present is worse than useless if it is given grudgingly.

To receive a present graciously, always open it when the giver is with you. Always show enthusiasm and try and engage with the giver beyond a simple thank you. If appropriate, ask them pertinent questions about the present, or muse on when you will use it. Disappointment, distaste or just indifference must be hidden at all costs. For all but the most casually given gifts, a written thank you is appropriate.
See also Christenings; Engagement; Re-Gifting; Wedding Lists

PRONUNCIATION

If someone mispronounces a word it is very rude to correct
their pronunciation – they will feel crushed and foolish.
The tactful option is to reintroduce the word that has been
mispronounced into the conversation: by using the correct
pronunciation you will be alerting them to the mistake; they
can either choose to rectify their error in future, or stick
doggedly to their own version.

While everyone admires linguistic ability, you should
restrain any desire to show off your skills by over-
pronouncing foreign words. Generally, if foreign words
are used in English conversation they are gently anglicised;
guttural or phlegmatic consonants, trilled 'rs' and
exaggerated glottal stops are unnecessary and obtrusive.

PROPOSAL, MARRIAGE

'Grow old with me! The best is yet to be.'
ROBERT BROWNING

A proposal of marriage requires planning. It's an occasion
that demands once-in-a-lifetime romance that will be
recalled time and time again, so it is important to get it
right. The location should be memorable and the timing
should be carefully thought through.

It is traditional for a man to propose with a ring, but
not strictly necessary. Some women prefer to choose one
together; in that case, a piece of jewellery should be given
instead, such as a bracelet. A ring should, however, be on
her finger within a reasonable time of her saying 'yes'.

It's not compulsory for the man to get on one knee, but most women will appreciate it. He must sound confident and clear when he pops the question – she doesn't want to be guessing if she's heard correctly. If the answer is 'yes', celebrations will inevitably follow. If she says 'no' then she should offer to give the ring back – it's up to the man if he wants to take it or not. Equally, if she doesn't like the ring that's been chosen, she should gently and tactfully tell him, as she'll be wearing it forever. *See also Engagement*

P'S AND Q'S

Opinions differ as to the origin of the phrase, 'p's and q's'. Some say that it was once shouted in pubs when things were getting a little rowdy, "Mind your Pints and Quarts!", these being the main measurements of drinks before the Second World War. Others say that it was an old printer's axiom; a reminder to typesetters to pay attention to the details.

Regardless of its origins, this admonition has been common in post-Victorian Britain as an abbreviation of 'to mind your manners' or, more specifically, to say both 'please' (p's) and 'thank-you' (thank-q's). This is inevitably a child's very first introduction to manners, and parents are haunted by the mantra-like repetition of, "Say please/ thank-you!" every few minutes for the first five, ten or fifteen years of their child's existence. In this case, the tedium of repetition is surely justified – a child who doesn't mind their p's and q's, the most basic of good manners, is being given a very poor start in life.

PUBLIC TRANSPORT

Basic courtesies are easily forgotten on public transport, particularly if delays are lengthy and space is tight. Do not perpetuate this. Always offer your seat to those who need it more than you do. If pregnancy or decrepitude are in any doubt, it is best to quietly vacate your seat, move away and hope that your intended recipient will gravitate towards it. Remember that proximity heightens tension and amplifies your behaviour, so be considerate if using a mobile phone, eating, drinking, listening to music or carrying outsized luggage. If a fellow passenger wrongs you, ignore it and avoid confrontation. Smile and thank others who show forbearance or gestures of goodwill, including the driver and any staff. *See also Eating in Public; Headphones; Quiet Zones; Trains*

PUBS

'Few things are more pleasant than a village graced with a good church, a good priest and a good pub.'
JOHN HILLABY

Observe and respect the atmosphere you find in a pub. If your fellow drinkers are sitting alone or in couples quietly chatting and reading papers don't ruin the mood with loud banter or uproarious games of darts and pool. Likewise, if you are in a busy town-centre pub after work on a Friday there's no point complaining about the rowdy group of office-workers letting their hair down at the table next to you. Pubs are very sociable places so be prepared to exchange small talk with strangers.

If a group of you are drinking together it is usual for people to take it in turns to buy a round. Don't opt out of rounds, or hang back; you shouldn't have to be asked. Tipping is not necessary in a pub. However, if you feel you've received particularly notable service you may like to offer the bar staff a drink. *See also Bars*

PUNCTUALITY

'I have always been a quarter of an hour before my time, and it has made a man of me.'
LORD NELSON

Failing to be punctual is the height of bad manners because it disregards the value of other people's time. By being late you are effectively forcing the people you are meeting to waste their time; hanging around waiting for someone is deeply frustrating. By being late, you will always arrive at your rendezvous on the wrong foot; flustered, apologetic, disadvantaged. Conversely, being punctual always scores bonus points. You will come across as someone who cares about other people, and is efficient, organised and reliable.

Given the vagaries of transport systems, the tendencies of meetings to over-run, the unpredictable emergencies of modern life, you cannot expect to be invariably punctual. If you see that you're going to be late, pre-empt the fallout, and call the person you're meeting to tell them, with profuse apologies, that you are delayed. If the situation looks out of control (total rail shutdown, terrorist alert, home emergency), inform them immediately and reschedule.

PUNCTUATION

Punctuation isn't voluntary. Full stops, commas, colons and so on are the only things that stand between cogent prose and stream-of-consciousness anarchy. Don't be fooled by the language of modern texting and emailing into thinking that punctuation can be dispensed with. If you don't punctuate your prose adequately, and correctly, it will be opaque, open to misconstruction and confusing. Punctuation is frequently dismissed as the preserve of the pedantic and old-fashioned, but it is, first and foremost, an indispensable tool. Use it wisely. *See also Email; Grammar*

QUAILS' EGGS to QUITTING

QUAILS' EGGS

These tiny speckled eggs are usually served hard-boiled
in their shells, with celery salt on the side. Gently peel off
the shell, dip into the salt and eat in a delicate bite or two.

QUEEN, HM THE

A formal encounter with The Queen will be intricately
organised and choreographed, so you should wait to be
presented rather than initiate an introduction. Men
should bow from the head only, and women should make
a small curtsey. Neither movement should be prolonged
or exaggerated. It is acceptable but less usual to shake hands.

Address The Queen as 'Your Majesty' and subsequently
as 'Ma'am' (to rhyme with 'jam'). As far as conversation is
concerned, you may be briefed in advance as to how much
time is available. However, allow yourself to be guided
during the audience itself. Relax and behave as naturally
as possible. If you are introducing another person to
The Queen, simply state the name of the person as follows:
"May I present John Smith, Your Majesty?" When conversing
with The Queen, substitue 'Your Majesty' for 'you'.

When writing to The Queen, address your letter 'Madam'
or 'May it please Your Majesty' and close with 'I have the
honour to remain, Madam, Your Majesty's humble and
obedient servant'. In the body of the letter, substitute
'Your Majesty' for 'you' and Your Majesty's' for 'your'.
The envelope should be addressed to 'Her Majesty
The Queen'. *See also Bowing; Curtseying; Ma'am; Royal Family*

QUERULOUSNESS

'Probably Providence has implanted peevishness and ill-temper in sick and old persons, in compassion to the friends or relations who are to survive; as it must naturally lessen the concern they might otherwise feel for their loss.'
LAURENCE STERNE

Maintaining an air of peevish irritability is the essence of bad manners. Your discontent will make your companions feel bad; they will either be infected by your complaints, or will be made to feel guilty for not sharing them. Minor inconveniences or discomforts should be confronted with robust good humour, not querulousness. If you are experiencing more severe diffculties, then a querulous complaint will only serve to undermine other people's estimation of the magnitude of your problems.

QUEUING

'An Englishman, even if he is alone, forms an orderly queue of one.'
GEORGE MIKES

Where other nationalities mass frenziedly, the British queue. Turn up at a railway station, or a supermarket, or a post office and you will see an orderly queue. It all dates back to the days of rationing in the long years during and after the World Wars of the last century, when queuing effectively meant the difference between an empty plate and a plate filled with the delights of powdered egg and leaden bread. In such dark days, the queue was an opportunity to catch up with the community, check that your friends were still alive and moan about the privations. Even today, grumbling in a queue is one of the great British joys. There is a liberating anonymity in conversing with someone whose back is to you; the grumbler in front will turn enough so that you can hear them but not enough so that you exchange eye contact and graduate to actual personal interaction and the implications of intimacy that this might entail.

For foreigners, the art of queuing must seem esoteric at best and maddening at worst: queue-barging is the worst solecism a foreigner can commit; even the reticent English will feel justified in sharply pointing out the back of the line to any errant queue-jumpers. But there is the finest of lines between queue-barging and proactive queuing – and anyone that isn't fully committed to moving forward an inch for every inch that opens up will earn the equal opprobrium of the crowd queuing behind. Wheelie suitcases are a new spanner in the works of the immaculate British queue; gaps cannot be closed sufficiently; bags that should be held in front or put on the ground and kicked forward are now loitering in such a way as to trip the unwary. But we can absorb such wrinkles into our queuing science: for nothing can sully the joy of being in the queue (say, at passport control or at the supermarket) that beats another queue. Such moments of pure adrenalin are what life is all about.

QUIET ZONES

A designated 'quiet zone' is precisely what it says. Don't abuse your fellow passengers by engaging in mobile phone

chats, or loud conversations in these zones. If someone else is doing the talking, politely point out the sign to them, prefacing your remark with a deprecating "I'm sure you haven't noticed the sign but . . .". If they still transgress, inform a member of staff, and wait for them to be removed.
See also Mobile Phones; Public Transport; Trains

QUITTING

It's something you can't go back on, so it's worth getting it right. Managing your resignation from a job must be done as carefully as you would handle any other business endeavour; no matter how tinder-dry those bridges, you will regret any arsonist impulses. Of course, the compulsion to quit spectacularly, sweeping into your boss's office and telling them exactly what you think of them, is sometimes strong; but such sweet revenge soon sours. Even if you hate your boss, be kind and positive when you quit: for they are no longer your boss of the past but part of your network of the future.

People tend to remember just their first and last impression, so be professional, don't say too much, emphasise the positive about your time in the company but add that it's time to move on, you've found an opportunity that 'fits you better'. Offer to help during the transition; seeking out or training up your replacement. Whatever the job, accompany any spoken intent with a formal letter of resignation stating when your last day will be; it looks more professional, and will clear up any uncertainties about

notice periods. This way, you will leave the job, but not shut the door on that part of your life.

Quitting properly is also a transferable skill — it can be applied not just to jobs, but to relationships and voluntary responsibilities that suddenly become too much ... your child's school PTA, that charity committee. Any gathering of voluntary workers is not just beset by petty politics and, all too often, absurd rivalries, but is also notoriously difficult to extricate yourself from. It may be tempting to invent or embroider a family crisis, illness, or to plump for the usual 'stress' excuse, but simply following the job-quitting model can often work better. Again, don't go into detail, just say that you're resigning, either directly to your manager or in writing, and give the last date you will be available for help. If pressed to give a reason, just shake your head mournfully, smile wistfully and murmur about it being 'time'; this way, dignity is upheld, mystery created. Job well done!

RACISM TO RSVPS

RACISM

In these days of migration, inter-marriage and cross-cultural interaction, race is an elastic and fluid concept. To attempt to define, or worst of all stereotype, a person or group according to their so-called race, is clearly a gross oversimplification, and betrays a terrible, and dangerous, lack of imagination – the blinkered tendency to view other people through the lens of one's own sense of entitlement and 'superiority'.

This is a highly charged area, and it's advisable to step with care. Never, ever dismiss a person as being 'typical' of a certain racial group. Never associate negative traits with one racial entity. Strive, always, to relate to the person, not to the collection of attributes that you think they represent.

If you witness someone else being racist, you may feel confident enough to point this out. If you don't, you can always counteract with humour: an off-the-cuff riposte, or amusing put-down. If you're not feeling sufficiently quick-witted, then a totally blank response is your best weapon; an ill-chosen remark will resonate, embarrassingly, if it is met with silence. *See also Xenophobia*

RECYCLING

With apocalyptic studies on the environment published every week, the pressure to recycle has never been greater. Even if you are sceptical of threats of global warming, recycling household items is so straightforward that you should make the effort. If you don't find the evidence compelling, consider the social motivation. Appearing overly blasé about environmental concerns can make you appear self-centred and lacking in foresight. An impressive array of recycling boxes, on the other hand, will be applauded. Few homes are without doorstep collection facilities, but the vagaries of council policies can still leave you with a space-consuming stash. A monthly trip to a recycling centre will salve your conscience and avoid raised eyebrows among your more socially responsible neighbours. *See also Eco-Etiquette; Environment, Respecting*

REFUSING

'The only man who is really free is the one who can turn down an invitation to dinner without giving any excuse.'
JULES RENARD

Refusing graciously, without causing offence, is a vital social skill. Whatever the occasion — a date, a dance, an invitation — you have the right to turn the offer down, and on many occasions you will be genuinely unable to accept because of previous commitments. Whether you are truly already committed, or simply indifferent to the invitation, good manners demand that you offer up some sort of excuse. Simply saying "No, thank you" seems distressingly bald; indicating that you have, for example, a prior (or imminent) engagement softens the blow. Do not, however, make the mistake of buttressing your refusal with elaborate excuses. Less is more, and over-embroidering will instantly rouse suspicion.

If you really don't want to comply (an importunate suitor, for example) a point-blank refusal will certainly get the message across: there will be occasions when you are confronted with a relentless inability to read social signals — and at that point, your good manners may have to be compromised.

RE-GIFTING

It's an ugly portmanteau of a word, but re-gifting is the art of passing on something given to you to someone else. It is practical and admirable in this world of excess and obsolescence to recycle in this way; how much better to cut down on all the disposable detritus and make two, or even three or four, people happy into the bargain? The theory is marvellous, but the practice has to be watertight. No one must ever know: not the original giver nor the next-in-line receiver. They may find this admirable theory harder to swallow if they're the one whose gift is being spurned or the one being palmed off with second-hand goods. So ensure that receiver is at least six degrees separated from the giver, and that the 're-gift' is shop fresh and unmarked (snagged threads or notes in the margin might just be a giveaway). Check the present has not been personalised in any way by the original giver — you'll be mortified if on p.235 of that re-gifted hardback, there's a note saying, "I knew you'd love this bit, Lucy!" and you've just given it to Fred.

Finally, be careful not to crow too much — never tell anyone about your penchant for re-gifting (from then

on they'll never give you anything and will be perennially suspicious about their own presents from you) – and don't present the re-gift with too much fanfare. Just in case. Because recycling and planet-saving are all very well, but deep down, you know that what you are doing is ... cheap.
See also Presents

RELIGION

'There are no aetheists on a turbulent aircraft.'
ERICA JONG

Religion is an issue that affects everyone – and on which no one person can persuade us all to agree. There are, obviously, codes of behaviour particular to each religion: suffice to say the best approach is to tread carefully, respect all differences and adjust your own behaviour to suit the context in which you find yourself. If travelling in a Muslim country, for example, respect more conservative dress codes, especially for women. Always treat monks, imams, rabbis with politeness and respect. Dietary restrictions should be taken seriously and accommodated.

When it comes to your own social life, however, it is somehow harder to observe the same sensitivities. When your hitherto louche and amusingly debauched friend welcomes you with a suspiciously open smile and announces that he has found Jesus and he wants to bring you to find Jesus too, proceed with sensitivity. It is all too simple to mock the born-again Christian – the easy talk of love and redemption, the prayerful demeanour – but to do so is to push against an open door. Is it good manners to mock people who have been taught to turn the other cheek and, however unfashionably, have rediscovered the art of being nice to the people around them? Cynicism can cast one in an unflattering light and makes one look, quite simply, rude. Be friendly towards the Jehovah's Witness, the Hare Krishna monk, the born-again, and you might actually learn something from listening for five minutes. After all, it might just be worth hedging your bets – like Bob Hope who said, 'I do benefits for all religions. I'd hate to blow the hereafter on a technicality.'

RESTAURANTS

'Dining out' describes a plethora of eating experiences, but restaurant rules are universal. Although you are the customer, a little charm goes a long way. Treating your waiter or waitress respectfully will enhance your experience no end, but attempting to befriend them is inappropriate; you should allow serving staff to do their jobs discreetly. Whenever possible, make a reservation; always book if you are dining in a group, and discuss any special requirements with the restaurant in advance. If you are unhappy with the table you are allocated, ask whether it is possible to be accommodated elsewhere, but do this before you sit down to minimise disturbance. If the waiter assists a woman in taking her seat, she should accept the offer graciously, and wait until the chair is touching the back of her knees before beginning to sit down.

If you are hosting a gathering, it is perfectly acceptable to take control of the wine list, but defer to anyone who demonstrates an intimate knowledge of the cellar. When dining *à deux*, share the responsibility and make the selection a talking point. Many restaurants now offer tap, as well as bottled, water. There is no shame in requesting it.

When dining in a group, you should try to agree collectively on the number of courses. Once you have chosen, close your menu. If you know that someone else will be picking up the bill, choose modestly. If you are footing the bill, you should suggest to your guests that they have free rein. Men should no longer expect to order for women; they should do so only if there is a specific request.

Normally, everyone at the table is served at the same time. Wait until all dishes have arrived at the table before starting. If yours is lagging behind, insist the others start, and wait a few minutes before quietly enquiring as to where yours is. If you are dissatisfied with the food, say so discreetly and with minimal fuss, and request any necessary (and reasonable) changes. Keep things pleasant, and don't shoot the messenger. Be aware that voluble complaints may spoil your companions' evening.

If the event has been organised by you, it is your responsibility to pay (unless another arrangement has been agreed beforehand). If the bill is to be split, divide it equally; niggling about the comparative cost of dishes and drinks will look cheap. Always leave an appropriate tip, except when service has been exceptionally poor. *See also Bill, Paying the; Complaining; Going Dutch; Tipping*

ROAD RAGE

'Anybody going slower than you is an idiot and anybody going faster than you is a maniac'.
GEORGE CARLIN

Until you've learned to drive, you've never really learned true fury. On the road, it is all too tempting to succumb to road rage – you need to be somewhere fast and you are justified in feeling a little annoyance when seemingly every other road-user is intent on delaying you. But road rage will do nothing to speed up the journey and reduces the driver to an impotent, gibbering wreck. Seen through the silencing layers of car windows, the enraged driver – pop-eyed, bulging-veined and purple-faced – simply looks ridiculous. Be careful about chuckling at the transgressor. Road rage is increasingly no laughing matter, with people now being beaten up, dragged out of their car or even murdered. It may be tempting to wag your finger in a schoolmarm-ish way at a road-rager just for the pleasure of winding them up into incandescent fury but do remember that your car is not an impervious bubble, and that road rage can quickly become actual bodily harm.

When you have incurred fury in another driver either don't react at all or just smile and mouth, "Sorry!" repeatedly. Road rage is now being joined by air rage, pavement rage, parking place rage, train rage, even school drop-off rage. In this ever-crosser world, our need to handle ourselves around the boiling pots of fury that are our fellow citizens has never been greater. Drive carefully is now an adage for all walks of life. *See also Anger; Driving; Zebra Crossings*

ROUND ROBINS

Most usually included in Christmas cards, round robin
newsletters are best avoided. They are impersonal and can
seem boastful, especially if they are a rambling litany of the
family's achievements. Instead, include a short, personal
letter with cards to friends or relatives who are rarely seen.

ROYAL ASCOT

The dress code for racegoers is clearly prescribed and
will vary depending on the area of the course you will
be frequenting. For general admission, smart attire is
expected. Ladies' hats are not obligatory but they add to
the sense of occasion. For men, it goes without saying that
jeans, sportswear and shorts are not permitted. If entering
the Royal Enclosure you should dress with appropriate
formality. Ladies must wear a hat, and shoulders and midriff
should not be on display. Men must wear black or grey
morning dress with a waistcoat. A top hat must be worn
throughout the Royal Enclosure, except in a private box.
See also Hats, Morning Dress

ROYAL FAMILY

There is no accepted code of behaviour for encounters with
royalty, but adhering to the traditional forms of address will
prevent anxiety. When meeting any member of the Royal
Family, men should bow from the neck, and women should
make a small curtsey. A handshake is also acceptable. For

male members of the Royal Family, use 'Your Royal Highness' and subsequently 'Sir'. A female member of the Royal Family – except The Queen – should be addressed as 'Your Royal Highness' followed by 'Ma'am'.

Should you happen upon a member of the Royal Family during their time off, allow them the freedom to go about their business as an ordinary person. Assume that to royalty, being left alone is far from a discourtesy; it is a luxury.
See also Bowing; Curtseying; Ma'am; Queen, HM The

RSVPS

Reply to invitation promptly and use the correct medium. If you received an invitation by post it is appropriate to send a handwritten reply; if someone has invited you by email you can reciprocate; if a phone number is given, it is acceptable to call. If you have been invited to a big event, such as a wedding, a reply card is often included so always use this to respond. If you'd like to add anything, such as an explanation as to why you can't attend the event, this should be done in a separate letter.

A reply to official functions and formal private invitations (including weddings) should be sent, if possible, on headed writing paper and written in the third person. Address it to the hostess, even when the invitation is a joint one from both the host and hostess. State the name of any guests you are bringing if the invitation has been addressed to you 'and Partner' or 'and Guest.' Reiterate the date and time in the body of the letter. *See also Invitations; Debrett's 'Correct Form'*

SCRATCHING TO SWEARING

SCRATCHING

Wherever the itch may be, and however persistent or
irritating, it is totally unacceptable to scratch in public.
If you are being driven to distraction, make your excuses
and withdraw to somewhere private.

SEAT, OFFERING ONE'S

In the past it was always considered courteous for a man to
offer his seat to a woman. It is now a more tricky matter of
personal judgement. There is no need to jump up on the
train or underground every time you see a woman standing
(unless she is pregnant or elderly, when it is a definite
requirement). But if circumstances are particularly taxing
or uncomfortable, and you're feeling chilvalrous, you
should offer — she can always refuse. *See also Chivalry*

SEATING PLAN

A seating plan, or *placement*, is a good way of organising your
guests, but can look over-formal and seem intimidating.
If you're going for a more relaxed atmosphere don't plan
the seating arrangements; just make sure that couples are
separated and — if possible — genders alternate. Sit those
with similar interests together and balance loudmouths by
sitting them at opposite ends of the table. The host should
sit near the door/kitchen. Keep a close eye on proceedings
during the first couple of courses, pay particular attention
to guests who are shy or have come alone; if anyone is

looking bored to death or irritable you could suggest
a compulsory swapping of seats for pudding and coffee.

For official functions a seating plan is important. The
principal guest is placed on the host's right. Traditionally
the principal guest's wife would be placed on the host's left,
the host's wife being placed on the right of the principal
guest. For large gatherings such as weddings display a seating
plan with numbered tables and a list of guests at each table.

SECRETS

'Three may keep a secret if two of them are dead.'
BENJAMIN FRANKLIN

There are two kinds of secrets: confidences that are made
to you, in the course of normal conversations between
friends; and fully acknowledged secrets. Discretion must
be applied to confidences: they have been given to you
freely, and you have not been sworn to secrecy. There may
be occasions — perhaps when gossiping with friends — when
you feel an overwhelming urge to pass confidences on. You
should do so only after closely examining your motives (are
you using another person's secrets to curry favour? Is your
own social popularity riding on the back of a betrayal of
a close friend?). If you decide to go ahead with sharing the
confidence then you must make absolutely sure that this
decision will not rebound on you: you will not want to
be traced as the source of the 'leak'.

When, on the other hand, you are sworn to secrecy, you
are entering into a pact, and making an agreement — a social

contract – not to spill the beans. If you have any sense of honour or integrity, therefore, you will keep the secret at all costs. If you know that you are incapable of doing so, then you should say so. If you are an incorrigible blabbermouth you will miss out on one of life's great pleasures – the surreptitious thrill of shared secrets. *See also Whispering*

SEDUCTION, ART OF

'She's beautiful, and therefore to be wooed; She is a woman, therefore to be won.'
WILLIAM SHAKESPEARE

If you are planning a seduction in advance, tailor your strategy around the object of your desire. To be a successful seducer you must understand their desires, not ride roughshod over them. They may see a rakish lothario as an embarrassing nightmare, or turn into putty in the hands of an earnest, serious-minded suitor. Respect their right not to turn to jelly in the face of your charms; avoid acquiring the unfortunate reputation of a player, or worse, by saving any overt seduction tactics for when you really mean it.

Above all, ensure that you are comfortable with your technique. Setting your stall out as a one-night-only Don Juan or dominatrix is doomed to fail if you are generally more restrained in everyday life. Remaining true to yourself is especially important if you have designs on a longer term liaison. Even if you do not, a little decorum will ensure that you look back on your antics with a wry smile rather than a blush and a groan of dismay. *See also Flirting; Making a Pass*

SELF-RIGHTEOUSNESS

We live in a world of polarised moral absolutes – the religious fundamentalist, the committed Socialist, the ruthless capitalist, the earnest eco-warrior – all of whom think that they occupy the moral high ground. For those of us sandwiched in the middle, it is sometimes hard to hear anything other than the clamour of the righteous. Even if we stray away from the strictly moral, there are so many new ways to be self-righteous – about breastfeeding or natural childbirth, about composting or carbon footprints, about Third World Debt or Western interventionism. The mystery is, why, when the causes are so unimpeachable, is the self-righteousness so unattractive and, even more devastating, so ineffective?

Perhaps real conviction has a softer, more persuasive voice than the shrill hue and cry of righteousness. If you're ever tempted to be a little self-righteous, or start to hear that sharpness creep into your voice and mind, just ask yourself whether self-righteousness ever actually charmed anyone into changing their mind. More often than not it will drive its targets into contrary wilfulness. Few things are harder to put up with than the annoyance of being set a good example; your ex-smoker friend's self-righteous little hand-waggles as he waves away your smoke just make you want to blow smoke rings in his face.

If you are intent on saving the world and everyone in it, just bear in mind that self-righteousness will get you nowhere – don't wear your cause on your sleeve but tucked firmly away in an inside pocket.

SELFISHNESS

'To love oneself is the beginning of a lifelong romance.'
OSCAR WILDE

The me-me-me generation has elevated ego to the exclusion of all else, lending selfishness a patina of respectability. We now know all about our rights and correspondingly less about our responsibilities; the sharp-elbowed and selfish seem to be inheriting the earth at the expense of the meek and unselfish.

It is a pious truism to point out that looking out for yourself is a lonely and unfulfilling mission. More importantly, evolution is not about the survival of the species, but about the survival of the individual, the gene; an end which is inherently selfish. So to some extent – when we are fighting for the rights of our children to a decent education, or our parents to competent healthcare – we have to be selfish, and there is no point pretending otherwise.

Instead, aim to transcend our selfish genes little by little. It may be unrealistic to aim for a Mother Teresa-style selflessness, but just try to add something unselfish to each day – one act of kindness, or one less selfish act.

SEXISM

'Excellence is the best deterrent to any 'ism'.'
OPRAH WINFREY

We've come a long way since the days when Nietzsche wrote, 'Woman was God's second mistake', but the Battle of the Sexes is still being waged. There are still glass ceilings in place, especially for those who come back from maternity leave to find that their prospects are diminished. There is still a risible number of female MPs, and the majority of top execs are male. Across the board, women earn less than their male counterparts, and are penalised for prioritising family over career. Sexism is rife in the attitude towards ageing: older men's faces are seen as 'distinguished', women's as 'wrinkled'. Women are ruthlessly judged by their appearance. Men are now delighted that their partners work and pull their weight in joint finances – but many still expect their dinner to be cooked for them at the end of both their working days.

But the scales are tipping and sexism is no longer exclusively a term applied to the behaviour of men towards women. Sexism cuts both ways. Is it not sexist that absent fathers must pay an arm and a leg in child support but absent mothers do not? That divorce law overwhelmingly favours the mother, no matter what the individual circumstances? There is an increasing need to avoid the knee-jerk retreat into 'isms'. So the next time you're bridling at some sexist treatment, stop to consider whether you've been sexist yourself lately in some of your assumptions ... and then calm down. There are bigger fish to fry than the odd sexist comment or gender stereotyping. *See also Feminism*

SEXUAL INNUENDO

The use of sexual innuendo has been a source of constant pleasure to writers throughout the centuries. The quality of wordplay has been decidedly up and down during that time, with only cunning linguists able to stay on top of the subject. Coming at innuendo too early in social intercourse can be a mistake – as can banging it out too quick and fast – and novices can often miss the full thrust of the point entirely. If you hit the spot, innuendo can be the climax of good manners – as in the exchange between a departing guest, "Thank you for having me!" and his hostess, "Thank you for coming!" Generally, however, restraining the urge to double all your entendres is usually the way to please your peers; in the end, sexual innuendo is rather exhausting ...

SHOOTING

A day's shooting is based on drives where the beaters (also known as drivers) flush out the birds for the guns (people shooting). It is important to remember that shooting is a dangerous activity, so know the local rules and obey them.

Don't make the mistake of claiming expertise that you don't have – shooting is too dangerous for vanity. If you are inexperienced, or a first-timer, own up. It's perfectly acceptable to bring a mentor, such as a shooting instructor.

Wrap up warm and try to be waterproof. Wellington boots, a wax or quilted jacket, and a tweed hat or fedora are essential. Always point a gun downwards, carry it 'broken' and never point it at anyone or anything apart from the sky or the ground. Always make sure there is sky behind a bird when you shoot, and never shoot low birds or anything at close range.

Don't use your mobile phone and don't talk during drives; at the end of a drive, the beaters will announce "All Out!". The 'bag' is the number of birds killed that day; two birds are referred to as a brace. Tip the gamekeeper generously when you shake his hand at the end of the day and write a prompt letter of thanks to your host.

SHOPPING

Whether traipsing the high street or scouring the internet, our retail appetites are insatiable. While online shopping liberates us from the shackles of social interaction, many still prefer the old-fashioned method. Your behaviour should remain the same regardless of your destination, but you may wish to consider your attire – if you know you will be breezing around the smarter end of town, it doesn't hurt to dress the part.

Don't be intimidated by those establishments that treat you dismissively. You are the customer, and must be treated with respect – they will be the losers if their insolence discourages a potential sale. Shop staff who talk amongst themselves as they serve you are simply being rude, and you are justified in complaining. On the other hand, you should never treat shop staff dismissively; mind your manners and you should find that you are rewarded with excellent service.

Shopping can and should be enjoyable. When it becomes unduly arduous, abort the mission if it's non-essential. You will probably buy the wrong thing and irritate yourself and others in the process. *See also Supermarkets*

SHYNESS

'The shy man does have some slight revenge upon society for the torture it inflicts upon him. He is able, to a certain extent, to communicate his misery. He frightens other people as much as they frighten him. He acts like a damper upon the whole room, and the most jovial spirits become, in his presence, depressed and nervous.'
JEROME K. JEROME

While shyness can be crippling in the young, it has a shelf-life. The sheer terror of social interaction for children or young people can be strong enough to induce debilitating physical symptoms – blushing, shaking, stammering, sweating hands, even the welling up of tears – but research has shown that this is more to do with the lack of social skills, the unfamiliarity of the situation and the anticipation of that unfamiliarity than with a deeper form of introspection or social anxiety. While it seems like a character trait, it is more often just a symptom of the fear of the unknown.

In other words, ordinary shyness can be conquered by simply putting yourself into timidity-inducing scenarios and forcing yourself to join in; however terrible it feels the first time, the second time will be exponentially better. Parents of naturally shy children are pivotal in influencing which way that shyness will go – gently handled and carefully introduced into non-threatening gatherings where they can develop their social skills at their own pace, these children will gradually shrug off their shyness. But if parents constantly excuse their children in front of others, "I'm sorry, little Charlotte is awfully shy" or actively tease or criticise them for their shyness, "See how Charlotte

blushes!" and do nothing to soothe the underlying anxiety, then they should not be surprised when the shyness escalates to crippling proportions.

Beyond the age of about thirty, however, shyness becomes less excusable. It can be used as a tool by the arrogant or lazy to dodge the need to interact with people. That person who tells you that they hate going to drinks parties because they are too shy to talk to people may be inadvertently confessing that they are too idle to make the effort.

Shyness in adults can also be a manifestation of acute self-consciousness, a painful hypersensitivity to the scrutiny of other people. As such, it is intensely egotistical. Conquer it by turning your attention away from yourself and focusing instead on the people around you; remember that you are not the fulcrum of every social interaction, but a small cog in the wheel. By protecting yourself behind a shield of good manners you will find an antidote to your shyness.

SILENCES

Not all silences are golden. On occasions, a discreet silence can serve a number of positive functions: signalling acquiescence, compliance, agreement. But silence can also be used as a weapon, a means of indicating disagreement, outrage or lack of cooperation. The context is critical.

Silences are, rightly, considered potent conversational tools; use them with discretion. If you are silent, you may make the people around you uncomfortable. Some people find silence intolerable, and will strive to fill the vacuum —

the silent treatment, aimed at a compulsive chatterer, is an act of outright aggression. Never confuse small conversational hiatuses with true silence: conversation is not invariably fluid, and short pauses are normal. Prolonged silences, on the other hand, are pregnant with meaning. *See also Pregnant Pauses*

SMART CASUAL

This dress code requires that you look smart but not overly formal. Men should wear a jacket or blazer and flannels or chinos, not jeans. A shirt and tie can be worn but an open collar is also acceptable. Women should be smart in a dress or skirt and top with a jacket. Avoid sportswear and wear smart shoes, not trainers. But don't be too formal; hats and gowns will look out of place. *See also Lounge Suits; Underdressed*

SMILING

'Wear a smile and have friends; wear a scowl and have wrinkles.'
GEORGE ELIOT

All too often smiling provokes cynicism, because it is used to mask negativity. The vulpine smile of the salesman as they hover on the edge of a deal, the insincere grimace of the flight attendant as they dole out another hot meal, the meaningless teeth-baring of the customer service representative who has no intention of serving any customer; all these lend themselves to the 'villain, villain, smiling, damned villain' of Hamlet's rant. Even babies' smiles – hailed by their proud-as-punch parents as the first examples of their natural congeniality – have, in those under four months, been written off by killjoy scientists as merely 'a reflex making possible the rapid and effective expulsion of gas'.

Within the context of manners, smiling is often the armour of genial politeness we put on to see us through all sorts of social situations. As such, we could be accused of insincerity, but surely smiling is better, kinder, more attractive than the panoply of frowns, puzzlement, and boredom that might otherwise be the case. Remember that smiles are infectious – and spreading a little infectious happiness can only be a good thing. Be discerning; don't be surly at home, then go out in the street and waste your smiles on total strangers. Beware also of the fixed grin – in others, it presages anything other than happiness and in yourself, it can be interpreted only negatively as communicating displeasure, confusion, scorn or at best merely insincerity. To avoid the fixed grins forever immortalised in a million photo albums, don't ever say 'Cheese!'. Instead get your subjects to follow Cecil Beaton's advice and shout 'Lesbian!'.

SMOKING

If you are a smoker you will be feeling like a member of an endangered species, in more ways than one. Banned, excluded, hounded, disapproved of . . . these days an attachment to nicotine has to be very strong indeed if you are going to withstand the social pariah status of the smoker.

If you do smoke, try and do so considerately. Legislation has now taken much of this responsibility off your shoulders by simply prohibiting you from smoking in most public arenas. But when you find yourself huddled – with your co-smokers – outside the door of the pub, restaurant or office, be aware that cigarette stubs are a litter nuisance, and dispose of them carefully. Even in your own home you should always ask your guests "Do you mind if I smoke?". In other people's homes, you should offer to go outside – your host may take pity on you, especially on a cold and wintry night. Keep ashtrays clean, air smoke-filled rooms, launder smoke-infused clothes.

If you are a non-smoker, you should also try to behave with some tolerance. If people around you are doing their best to smoke discreetly and considerately, it is ill-mannered to complain, bat away the smoke from your nose, huff, mutter, ostentatiously cough, and so on. The huge efforts they are making (and being forced by law to make) to contain their addiction should be applauded, not derided.

SNAILS

Usually served by the half dozen and with their shells intact, snails require little manual dexterity to consume. The chances are that you will have the requisite utensils to hand. Grip the shell with the snail tongs, and remove the meat with the small two-pronged fork. Mopping up the juices with bread is acceptable, but in very formal company (or if in doubt), abstention is safer.

SNEEZING

A largely unavoidable interruption to proceedings, sneezing
is at the acceptable end of the bodily functions spectrum.
Always catch a sneeze in a handkerchief and be as discreet
as possible. Additional sound effects for emphasis should
be avoided. One or two sneezes is perfectly acceptable.
However, if you feel a sneezing fit approaching, remove
yourself from company where possible.

SNIFFING

Sniffing in public is unacceptable and should be avoided.
Carry a clean handkerchief or supply of paper tissues at all
times, and blow your nose when necessary. Should you find
yourself in the company of a sniffer, avoid the temptation
to offer them your handkerchief. If you find it unbearable,
remove yourself from the vicinity. *See also Nose Blowing*

SNOBBISHNESS

*'The true definition of a snob is one who craves for what separates
men rather than for what unites them.'*
JOHN BUCHAN

Snobs would claim that they are the guardians of civilisation,
the last bulwarks against the modern desire to become
inclusive, homogenous and bland. But a snob's very desire
to hold a clique together is divisive – and it is this negativity
that makes snobbishness so unattractive. A snob is someone
who is blinded to the natural charms of meeting someone

new because they are so busy making judgements about that person's accent, their taste, how they dress and where they went on holiday that year. Handling a snob can be difficult: their aim is to intimidate, which might make you defensive. But before you come out against their snobbery, all guns blazing, consider that it is often the case that the snobbier the person, the less socially secure they are. Armed with this magnanimous insight, you can afford to be a little kind and let them look down upon you to their heart's content. If criticising the way you speak, or dress, or work, or eat is how the snobs get their kicks, then leave them to it, and revel in a sense of genuine social superiority.

SOCIAL NETWORKING

The recent trend for social networking via websites has made new demands on traditional etiquette. Play it safe, and always employ your usual good manners when online, treating others with kindness and respect.

Remember, it's not a competition to see how many friends you can get. Think carefully before you accept someone or remove someone as a friend. Don't annoy your friends by constant, frantic poking.

Don't let social networking take over all other methods of communication. There are times when letters and phone calls are still important. It is always better to send birthday cards rather than a message on a networking site. Call your friends to tell them important news rather than posting an announcement online.

Think carefully about the photos you post, both of yourself and others. Consider your friends' feelings. Would they be happy for everyone to see the unflattering picture of them after their fourth tequila shot? Think about what your profile picture says about you, and don't fall into the trap of turning the online universe into a fantasy world, where you are more attractive and successful than in real life. Social networking is meant to complement and enhance your existing social life, not completely obliterate it. *See also Online Manners*

SOUP

Push your soup spoon from the front of the bowl away from you to catch a mouthful. Bring this to your mouth and tip the soup in from the side of the spoon; don't try eating with your spoon at 90 degrees to your mouth. Don't suck or slurp. Tilt the bowl away from you in order to get the last few spoonfuls. Put your spoon down while you break off pieces of bread. Leave your spoon in the bowl, not on the side plate, when you have finished. *See also Table Manners*

SPAGHETTI

This classic pasta dish should be served in a shallow bowl and accompanied by a fork only. Twist a small bundle of spaghetti around your fork by twirling it clockwise against the side of the dish. Never cut the threads of pasta with the side of the fork. Avoid splattering sauce, and never make slurping noises as you suck long strands of pasta into your mouth. Don't worry too much about the odd stray strand hanging from your mouth; short ones can be deftly drawn into your mouth and longer strands bitten off to drop onto your fork. Have a napkin handy!

SPEECHES

'It usually takes more than three weeks to prepare a good impromptu speech.'
MARK TWAIN

It may seem blindingly obvious, but deciding what you want to speak about is a vital first step. Having a clear topic, and focus, for your speech will make it far more arresting. Avoid inappropriate topics by thinking about the function of your speech: is it intended to amuse and entertain (after-dinner, wedding, special occasion); is it inspirational (political gathering); is it intended to exhort (sales conference etc.)? Think about your potential audience: their frame of reference, sense of humour, age, predominant gender — if you understand your listeners, your jokes, anecdotes and references will not fall on stony ground.

Next, research your topic thoroughly (never be caught out faltering, or uncertain of your facts). Write your speech down and ensure that it is well-paced: do not overload it with dense information, and jokes and anecdotes should be evenly dispersed. Practise your speech — preferably in front of a mirror or a willing friend — and time exactly how long it takes. Allow time for audience reaction.

When it comes to delivering your speech, do not read from the notes, but use them simply as an *aide-memoir*. Look up frequently, maintain eye contact with your audience, speak slowly, and pause if you are expecting a reaction. If you are dry-mouthed and nervous, do not worry about pausing to take a sip of water. Engage with your audience — you may be the only one speaking, but a good speech will elicit a response from your listeners. *See also Formal Dinners*

SPILLAGES AND BREAKAGES

It's almost *de rigueur* to fly into an extravagant panic when we spill wine on someone else's sofa or send a vase flying. But what's done is done, and it's the host's job to quell the furore and put a lid on the culprit's vociferous self-loathing. There are few stains that cannot be removed (there is invariably someone at a party who is an authority on stain removal). Breakages are more difficult to bear with equanimity. If you are responsible for either calamity, ensure that you offer to help clear the wreckage. Await guidance from the host or the injured party before weighing in with a napkin or dustpan and brush. After the clean-up, apologise sincerely and, if appropriate, offer to replace the item or pay for the damage. If you are on the receiving end of the apology, accept it graciously and decline payment.

If nobody witnessed the drama, it is imperative that you own up. Covering your tracks is the height of bad manners and will guarantee that if you are discovered, you will be consigned to the social wilderness.

SPITTING

Never spit in public. Professional sportsmen were once
forgiven for spitting on the pitch, but television close-ups
have made even this exception off-limits.

SPORTSMANSHIP

*'Serious sport has nothing to do with fair play. It is bound up with
hatred, jealousy, boastfulness, disregard of all rules and sadistic pleasure
in witnessing violence. In other words, it is war minus the shooting.'*
GEORGE ORWELL

Despite the antics of professional players the world over,
sport isn't just about winning the game, it's about playing
well. This means being magnanimous in victory, and
gracious in defeat. Sportsmanship is no more than good
manners: congratulating your opponents on effective play,
accepting the decisions of the referee/umpire with good
grace – absolutely no whining, arguing, sulking or
triumphal strutting. As an effective sportsman, you will
always have a highly developed sense of competition;
as a good sportsman, you will never let competitiveness
debase your conduct. *See also Gamesmanship*

STANDING, FOR A LADY

A man should stand up to greet a woman when she enters
the room for the first time. There is no need, however,
to jump up and down like a jack-in-the-box every time
she goes to the loo, gets a drink and so on. *See also Chivalry*

STRESS
Irritability, insomnia, inability to concentrate, smoking, drinking, nail-biting — the list goes on and on. For many of us, the symptoms of stress are overwhelming and hard to control. But stress is never an excuse for bad manners. So examine your behaviour, and try and deal with your stress before it takes over. Don't expect too much of yourself; find ways of relaxing; don't pile stress on stress; avoid too much alcohol; try and get plenty of sleep and eat well. If all else fails, go somewhere private, bite the pillow, shout and scream ... Then take a deep breath and reinstate your calm, social, well-mannered persona. Behaving well can be a very effective way of controlling stress.

STUBBLE
Men should be clean-shaven at all times. Stubble is the preserve of the young or exceptionally good-looking. It is not appropriate in most working environments and best avoided if it doesn't grow evenly. *See also Beards*

SUPERMARKETS
Crowded, noisy, confusingly full of choices, supermarkets can be an assault on the senses, which all too often turns into nerve-frazzling tension. Adopt good supermarket manners and you will avoid some of the worse symptoms of stress. Be a considerate trolley-pusher: negotiate your way carefully around obstacles; don't barge into other trolleys; don't leave

your trolley blocking the aisle as you forage on the shelves. Never stoop to trolley rage – the aggressive use of your trolley as a weapon to jostle and prod your fellow-shoppers is truly anti-social. Help elderly (or small) people to reach items on high, inaccessible shelves. Give other shoppers space; don't push or elbow your way to the produce. At the checkout, unload your shopping on to the conveyor, then place the divider ready for the next shopper. Don't leave your trolley lying about the car park, take it back to the designated area. *See also Shopping*

SUSHI

The preparation and consumption of sushi is highly ritualistic. Understanding the finer points of this may be unattainable for Westerners, but some basic principles should be observed. Miso soup is taken as a starter, straight from the bowl. Pour soy sauce into your saucer and mix in some wasabi. It is polite to pour your dining companions' sauce too. Dip sashimi (sliced raw fish on its own) into the sauce with your chopsticks and eat. Sushi rolls and nigiri (blocks of rice with fish on top) should be eaten whole; attempting to bite in two can lead to a scattering of debris across the table. It is not obligatory to use chopsticks when eating sushi, but it is always best to use them in formal company. When dinner is trundling past on a conveyor belt, ensure that you only take what you plan to eat. Forming a line of dishes is entirely unnecessary and waste is frowned upon. *See also Chopsticks*

SWEARING

'The foolish and wicked practice of profane cursing and swearing is a vice so mean and low that every person of sense and character detests and despises it.'
GEORGE WASHINGTON

In certain august establishments or in front of particularly severe personages, one can often be afflicted by a sudden giddy desire (similar to the vertigo that urges you to throw yourself off a high cliff) to say the F-word, just for the hell of it, just to bring some life to the buttoned-up souls around you. As the swear word leaves your lip, it may be an almost tangible speech bubble of energy but the trouble is that as it reaches the ears of your listeners, it has weakened into a foul little puff of pestilence. A conversation peppered with meaningless curses is one where both sense and expressive language is being diluted – how can you expect someone to respect what you are saying if you are distracting them with irrelevant swear words?

The acceptability of certain words has changed dramatically over the years, and today the line between a profane curse and an acceptable expletive has become blurred. The Victorian editor Thomas Bowdler 'bowdlerised' various famous works, carefully excising all sexual allusion and bawdy language (a 'bull' became a 'gentleman cow'). Now, at the other end of the spectrum, words like 'damn' and 'bloody hell' are seamlessly part of the argot where once they were fearsome curses. In some circles, swearing is now *de rigueur* – chef Gordon Ramsay defended his own dirty mouth by saying, 'Swearing is industry

language. For as long as we're alive it's not going to change. You've got to be boisterous to get results.' Everyday speech is infiltrated by vivid swear words of the Anglo-Saxon variety, and even the F-word is no longer bleeped out on post-watershed television.

Scientists have proved that swearing emanates from the lower brain, the part that processes emotion and instinct. Swearing is a motor activity, an automatic response to stress, pain and frustration. It is also a way of bonding with peers, and creating a group identity. It is often simply a habit.

Clearly this visceral habit has very little to do with good manners. Suppressing, or at the very least controlling, your worst language will have many benefits: you won't cause offence to others; you will be a better example to your children; you may even dream up some more linguistically creative ways of expressing rage and so on. Be aware of your swearing and keep your worst insults for life's most challenging situations – if every sentence is peppered with curses what will happen when you feel truly vituperative? Words will literally fail you . . .

TABLE MANNERS TO
TRUSTWORTHINESS

TABLE MANNERS

Dining politely should be second nature – or should at least appear to be. We all indulge in less-than-perfect behaviour in private, or in very familiar company, but some consistency at home and away will help you avoid the more heinous table offences.

The cardinal dining crime is eating noisily; nothing is more likely to get you noticed and promptly blacklisted. Keeping your mouth closed while chewing and taking care not to overfill it will enable you to breathe steadily. Eat at a relaxed pace and really think about your food. Not only does this make you appreciate what's on your plate, but it can also help you moderate your intake if you are so inclined. Wolfing down course after course will make you appear greedy. This is particularly important when dining *à deux*; your date will feel exposed if you gobble your food, put down your knife and fork and attempt full-throttle conversation while he or she is still eating. Talking while there is food in your mouth should be avoided at all costs – even when you have a conversational gem up your sleeve. Try to avoid directing a question at someone who is mid-mouthful, but don't despair if you mistime. A smile and an understanding nod will encourage them to swallow without rushing, spluttering or making sheepish gestures.

When dining in a group, always put others' needs before your own. Do your bit in offering communal dishes around the table, and hold them to assist your neighbour. If you are served a meal that is already on the plate, wait until everyone has been served before picking up your cutlery. Elbows should remain elegantly poised, but not resting on the table. Napkins should be dealt with as soon as you sit down, and placed on your lap — never tucked into the front of your shirt. Never gesture with your cutlery, and keep the tines of your fork facing downwards — unless it is your sole eating implement, in which case using it scoop-style is acceptable. Always move the soup spoon away from you, tipping the bowl in that direction, if necessary. Break off pieces of bread and butter them in bite-sized pieces. When you have finished, place your knife and fork — with the tines facing upwards — together on your plate.

If you are confronted with a plateful that is not to your taste, try to soldier on to avoid hurt feelings. Always attempt to sparkle conversationally, and don't monopolise one neighbour to the exclusion of another. Always compliment the cook. *See also Bread Rolls; Chewing; Cutlery; Napkins; Soup*

TABLE SETTINGS

The range of a cutlery arsenal will depend on the formality of the occasion, but the layout should always be the same — fork to the left, knives and spoons to the right and pudding implements above the place setting. A knife for buttering bread should be placed on or near the side plate, and to the left of the place setting. Simply work from the outside into the middle. Glasses should be placed to the right of the setting, and different glasses should be provided for red wine, white wine, water and, if you are serving it, champagne. Napkins should be folded simply; complex origami looks over-elaborate and should be avoided. Name cards are not necessary at casual gatherings, but it is the host's prerogative to seat guests where he or she thinks is most appropriate. Ensure that table decorations are lower or higher than eye level; being forced to peer around a floral display to make eye contact with the person opposite will inhibit conversation. *See also Cutlery*

TABOO TOPICS

When you don't know people well, it is advisable to avoid certain subjects: death, disease, religion, sexual orientation. In British society certain questions are also considered presumptuous: How much do you earn? Are you married? Why don't you have children? How much do you weigh? As you get to know people better, you will feel able to stray into more challenging territory, but always do so judiciously: be aware that some people are intensely private, and may well want to avoid discussing more intimate subjects.

TACT

'Talk to every woman as if you loved her, and to every man as if he loved you and… you will have the reputation of possessing the most perfect social tact.'
OSCAR WILDE

Tact is the delicate skill of handling a difficult situation and coming out with everyone still smiling. Tact is the ability to steer the rabid socialist away from the right-wing reactionary without either of them even knowing the other one was there. It is that quality that those of us, who come back from every party wracked with guilt about what we said/did/ danced, long to have. There is a hint of dishonesty in tact, but a little dash of duplicity is surely acceptable if it's to spare someone else's feelings or *amour propre*.

'Tact is the ability to describe others as they see themselves', wrote Abraham Lincoln; it is an unselfish art, where the tactful one removes himself or herself from the context to think only about others. By contrast, there is something selfish and thoughtless about being tactless: at best, an inability to avoid putting one's foot in it — at a cost to other people's feelings or sensibilities — or, at worst, a wilful ignorance about the effect your own words can have on others. 'A tactless man is like an axe on an embroidery frame', says an old Malay proverb — how much better to be the one who stitches a situation back together again.

TAXIS
When you see a taxi with its light on, i.e. available for hire, simply lift your arm and lean out from the pavement slightly to get the taxi driver's attention. Refrain from shouting 'Taxi' or waving frantically. Tell the driver your destination before getting in. Men should allow women to get in first; in London-style taxis women should take the banquette seat while men should take the fold-down seats if necessary. At your destination get out and pay the driver through the front window. The going rate for tipping is ten per cent.

A gentleman should always ensure his date gets home safely. Hail a taxi for her or, if sharing a taxi, try and arrange for the lady to be dropped off at her destination first.
See also Tipping

TEA

If serving tea for a group it is worth brewing a pot. Loose leaf tea will taste best. A second pot of hot water should be provided to dilute over-brewed tea if necessary. If a waiter places a teapot on the table without pouring the tea the person nearest the pot should pour for everyone.

Pour the milk and add the sugar before dispensing the tea. Lemons should be added afterwards. If the teapot contains loose tea, pour through a tea strainer. After stirring, remove the spoon from the cup and place it on the saucer. Hold the handle of the teacup between your thumb and forefinger; don't hold your little finger in the air.

Don't dunk biscuits in your tea unless in an informal setting, and don't slurp – even if it is piping hot.

TEASING

There is a fine line, when teasing, between that which is useful, constructive and amusing and that which is harmful, destructive and unfunny. Teasing is a great way of both showing your own wit and of cutting someone else down to size in a non-aggressive way – but for both, there are crucial parameters. The rule of thumb should be calibrated by how much the other person can take. If they are fabulously beautiful, popular and successful, they can – and should – take some teasing. If they are unconfident, marked out in some way by a physical defect or in any way trying to work their faltering way up through life, then the rule of thumb should be more generous: is it good manners to mock the afflicted? Even within a family, where teasing can run rampant, there are limits; as the inestimable Miss Manners points out, 'Family teasing is designed to take note of the successes and idiosyncrasies that make one beloved, not the traits that have been driving everyone crazy.' Tempting though it often is to play to the gallery, teasing should always be affectionately mindful of the target.

When being teased yourself, it is the hardest thing in the world to remain calm, good-natured and good-humoured, but you must. Your behaviour under the limelight of teasing will leave a longer-lasting impression than the teased-about defect. Better still is the ability to disarm teasing barbs with some related self-deprecation of your own, rather than outright denial or a knee-jerk counter-attack. Above all, don't take teasing too seriously: remember that it's intended more for others' benefit than as a genuine lesson for you.
See also Humour; Jokes

TEENAGERS

The chicken and egg conundrum fades into insignificance beside the problem of parents and teenagers. Which exacerbates the other? Pity the teenagers: their hormones are raging, their bodies are embarrassing them at every turn, they are neither adored children nor irreproachable adults and they need to sleep for 22 hours a day, which no one will let them do. Or pity the parents: their cherished little darlings have morphed overnight into hulking lumps of sullenness, who flinch at the sight of daylight and from whom their parents are lucky to extract the occasional grunt or uncooperative gesture.

As your 16-year-old would undoubtedly point out, why descend to the superficiality of judging teenagers more on their manners than on their character? As Somerset Maugham said, 'Few can suffer manners different from their own without distaste', so accept that normal teenagers are just differently mannered and swallow your distaste. Hail their occasional appearance during daytime hours with good grace, welcome every grunt as if it were the Sermon on the Mount and use humour to chip away at the seemingly unscalable wall between you and them. Your one weapon – and it must be used judiciously otherwise you will blunt its edge – is embarrassment, an emotion which dogs every teenager, every hour of the day. "Just joining in the fun," is a phrase to chill every teen's blood – try not to use it in front of their friends, merely threaten to use it in front of their friends if they don't cooperate at least one out of ten times.

The good news is that just as you might be feeling flabby and complacent in your chosen career, along comes a teenager to exercise your brain – the negotiating skills you will need when dealing with them will make years of study and work experience seem like a warm-up exercise…

TEXT MESSAGES

Text messaging is an acceptable form of modern communication but you must adhere to a basic code of texting conduct. Text messages are ideal for conveying a short, instant message. Don't use them to communicate important information or anything that needs a lengthy explanation. If you have to cancel an appointment, always make a phone call; apologies will be better received this way. Handwritten thank you letters should never be replaced by a text and never *ever* finish a relationship by text.

There's no need to use confusing, abbreviated text language. Use as much conventional grammar, spelling and punctuation as possible to make yourself clearly understood. The usual salutations and sign offs can be ignored.

Don't send or read text messages when you are out in company and turn your phone to silent when in a meeting or a 'quiet zone' on a train. Choose your text alert tone with care – a short bleep will suffice. *See also Mobile Phones*

THANK YOU NOTES/LETTERS

On receipt of a present, hospitality or some other kindness, you should always consider whether a note of thanks would be appropriate. Taking the time to write reassures the giver that their efforts are appreciated, especially if you talk around the subject – why you loved that particular present, what you most enjoyed about your visit, and so on. On those occasions when you are likely to receive a number of presents (a wedding or the arrival of a baby) make a note of who gave what and try to commit it to memory. It is embarrassing to thank someone effusively for the wrong gift. If you are genuinely pressed for time and have a huge number of people to write to, a generic thank you card is better than no acknowledgement at all. Notes should be sent as quickly as possible, but when it comes to saying thank you, better late than never is invariably the case.

THERAPY

'After a year in therapy my psychiatrist said to me, "Maybe life isn't for everyone".'
LARRY BROWN

Cognitive, Freudian, Jungian, relationship, lack-of-relationship, eating, not-eating, success, no success – there is therapy to suit every taste and every requirement. While it would obviously be simplistic to write off therapy as merely talking about oneself, there is nonetheless a danger that too much therapy can leave a person unattractively introverted in a social context – which is, perhaps, therapy speak for a 'self-obsessed bore'. For the greater good of mankind, it is marvellous that therapy is unlocking the doors to our repressed, embattled or self-harmed psyches but for the greater good of mankind's manners, it would be as well to remember that one's inner world should perhaps not be shared too much with the outer world. We can all recognise the danger signs – any sentence beginning with the words, "My therapist says I should . . .", and a liberal scattering of 'empowereds', 'inner children' and 'emotional journeys'.

Do not be lulled by the warm interest shown you by your therapist into thinking that your own emotional journey is as fascinating for others as it is for you – unless you're also planning to pay your friends for listening to you. If, on the other hand, you are faced with a friend who is determined to introduce you to their demons then tread carefully, for you tread on their dramas. Boring as it might be, you wouldn't be much of a friend if you didn't hear them out for as long as you can bear: it is, after all, probably part of their therapy to be able to talk about such things in public. So what if 'getting in touch with myself' translates in public as 'getting out of touch with everyone else'?

TIPPING

The practice of tipping varies from country to country according to legislation and the prevailing wage structure. Before travelling, it is worth consulting a guide book to ensure that you are familiar with the custom and do not cause offence. In the UK, tipping in restaurants is usually 'discretionary', but it is more discretionary in some places than others. Check your bill. 'Service not included' means just that, and it is usual to offer at least ten per cent. If you are paying by card, you will often be able to add the tip before entering your PIN number. This is fine, but leaving a cash tip is more likely to circumvent the odd unscrupulous proprietor and reach the waiting staff. Some establishments will add a discretionary percentage automatically. You are not obliged to pay this if service has been noticeably poor, and in some circumstances it is acceptable to ask for it to be removed. Tipping is also commonplace in hair and beauty salons and in hotels. Use discretion, but err on the side of generosity. *See also Bellboys; Hotels, Restaurants; Taxis; Valet Parking*

TITLES

People with titles do not necessarily use them in every situation, but it is safer to opt for formality, particularly when dealing with the older generation. It may take a little homework to ensure you get the title correct.

In correspondence use the full title on envelopes. When introducing peers or referring to them in conversation, a general guide is to use Lord and Lady in the same way as you would use Mr and Mrs. Do not use their descriptive title such as the Earl of Lonsdale or the Marquess of Bristol. The only exceptions are dukes and duchesses who are spoken to and referred to as the Duke and Duchess of Marlborough, for example, and addressed, in writing, as Duke and Duchess. *See also Debrett's 'Correct Form'*

TOLERANCE

'Tolerance implies no lack of commitment to one's own beliefs. Rather it condemns the oppression or persecution of others.'
JOHN F. KENNEDY

Tolerance in every definition (both the capacity to recognise and respect the beliefs of others and the capacity to endure hardship or pain) is at the very heart and soul of modern manners. George Eliot wrote that, 'The responsibility of tolerance lies with those who have the wider vision', and there is clearly still a need for that wider vision or education to be the seedbed of tolerance: you can't expect a toddler to be tolerant of someone taking his toys — he hasn't thought through the implications of sharing being a two-way street.

If faced with a lack of tolerance in someone else, the way of getting through that encounter with the least effect on one's blood pressure is to wonder if they are being so intolerant in this context because they are like that toddler — they haven't thought it through. That's not to say that one should tolerate intolerance silently (though in some circumstances it might be better to swallow what you were going to say and simply move on), but if you can persuade yourself that the intolerant one does not know what they are saying, it could make the conversation more peaceful and polite. Finally, tolerance does not imply weakness, so if tolerance means turning the other cheek or letting something slide over you like water off a duck's back, then do so knowing that it is done from a position of strength.

TOOTHPICKS

Toothpicks may be commonplace abroad, but they are not widely accepted here. Don't use toothpicks in public, and certainly not at the table, to remove food from between your teeth; do it somewhere private. If you are tempted to use a toothpick, never put it back on the table; hold on to it until you find somewhere where you can dispose of it.

TRAINS

*'Railway termini are our gates to the glorious and the unknown.
Through them we pass out into adventure and sunshine, to them, alas!
we return.'*

E.M. FORSTER

The weary stoicism of the British train traveller is legendary.
But basic good manners and respect for your fellow
passengers will go some way towards making even the
most crowded train journeys more tolerable.

Wait for other passengers to exit before boarding the
train: never jostle past people who are trying to get off.
Always give up your seat to someone who is elderly, disabled
or obviously pregnant. Mothers with small children in tow
should also be given priority. If necessary, help people to
put their luggage in the overhead racks. Some train carriages
are very quiet, packed with commuters reading newspapers
or working on their laptops, so be aware that loud mobile
phone conversations are very disturbing. If you are going
to listen to music on your MP3 player, ensure that you have
sound-proof headphones. Be aware that eating greasy,
smelly food (such as burgers) may well nauseate your fellow
passengers, and is a major cause of litter.

If the carriage is crowded don't take up an additional
seat with your excess baggage: you haven't paid for two
seats. Don't sprawl in your seat, or put dirty feet on the
seat opposite. Help people off the train with heavy baggage,
and put discarded newspapers, coffee cups and so on into
the bin – no one will want to sit surrounded by your
detritus. *See also Public Transport; Quiet Zones*

TRAVEL BORES

'The World is a book, and those who do not travel read only a page.'
SAINT AUGUSTINE

It is an unfortunate fact of life that, for some people, the book of their travels is all too thick. Travel bores are one of the unfortunate side effects of the travel revolution — where once, the tales of derring-do abroad of Golden Age explorers and discoverers could thrill for hours, now just the mention of a slide show or travel diary can chill the blood. The danger signs are clear: any hint of tie dye, more than the odd fetish or fertility figure on their mantelpiece, a marked tendency to frame their own photos in the entrance hall. 'Mind the Gap' should be an admonition to those returning from their gap year travels, armed with hilarious dysentery anecdotes and dramatic border-smuggling stories. Nowadays, we are all Raleighs, Marco Polos and Thesigers, no longer content to be mere tourists but vying with each other to have the most exotic, most dangerous, most bonding experience. The trouble is that, when traded indiscriminately, the currency of travel stories can become devalued, even worthless.

If you are brimming with travel anecdotes, mind that what you say is not just a rehash of what others have said before you; work out the attention span of your listeners; be aware that your audience may not be as wide-eyed and hungry for new experiences as you think they should be. Sometimes, travel bores are guilty of plain bad manners — like waxing lyrical about their eight months chilling-out in Asia to someone who has been working 60-hour weeks for the last two years; or banging on about the joys of hiking in the Rockies to someone with a wooden leg. Worse still, never overplay the lasting effect of your travels. No matter how many life-changing experiences we might have on our travels — and then want to talk about when we get back — we will not change the core of ourselves just because we have travelled. So settle back and enjoy your travels but don't expect that those who weren't there with you will want to share your journey ... *See also Bores, Escaping From*

TRUSTWORTHINESS

'A man who trusts nobody is apt to be the kind of man nobody trusts.'
HAROLD MACMILLAN

You will acquire a reputation as a reliable and trustworthy person if you follow these rules: do what you say you're going to do; never promise more than you can deliver; arrive on time; be meticulously honest in all your financial dealings; never reveal other people's secrets. Above all, never betray another person's trust. *See also Secrets*

U AND NON-U to UXORIOUSNESS

U AND NON-U

The expressions 'U' (Upper Class) and 'Non-U' (non-Upper Class) came to prominence in Nancy Mitford's *Noblesse Oblige* (1956). Although language is ever-evolving and society visibly relaxing, there are still certain words that may raise an eyebrow in status-conscious environments. Remember the basics: loo or lavatory never toilet; sofa never settee; napkin never serviette; supper never tea; drawing room or sitting room, never lounge or front room.

UNDERDRESSED

There are few things more uncomfortable than feeling underdressed for the occasion. It is always best to err on the side of formality; if you find you are overdressed, then a tie or jacket can be easily discarded. It is much harder to dress up a casual look, especially if you don't know the hosts well enough to borrow items of clothing. If you are unsure about the formality of an event, or worried about the dress code, check with the host beforehand – it is better to look over-anxious than underdressed. *See also Smart Casual*

UNDERSTATEMENT

A quality that is much revered – and exploited – by the British, understatement is frequently seen as being synonymous with good manners. Understatement is characterised by a number of negatives: a refusal to be effusive, overdramatic, emphatic or didactic. More direct remarks are frequently accompanied by tentative or provisional qualifications: 'perhaps', 'it could be', 'I wonder if', 'maybe'. The overall effect is an aura of modest reticence, quiet understanding and considerate behaviour. Like self-deprecation, understatement is an attractive and effective quality, which is often more persuasive, and appealing, than a direct approach.

Understatement permeates British humour; the unexpectedly low-key response to dramatic crises is a staple of the likes of Monty Python: when, for example, a bourgeois English dinner party is disrupted by a visit from Death, in the guise of the Grim Reaper, in *The Meaning of Life*, the classic response is 'Well, that's cast rather a gloom over the evening, hasn't it?'. *See also Ostentation*

UNDERWEAR

The appearance and condition of underwear is a private matter but well-maintained, and stylish, underwear can make a remarkable difference to the morale. Keep your underwear to yourself; avoid any unfortunate fashions that involve displaying your underwear – they are usually short-lived and will be regretted. *See also VPL*

URINALS

Always leave an empty urinal between you and the next man; if this is not possible, use the cubicle. Look straight ahead. Don't talk. Don't make eye contact. *See also Loo*

UXORIOUSNESS

'Uxoriousness, n. A perverted affection that has strayed to one's own wife.'
AMBROSE BIERCE

Of course, a man who dotes on his wife (or a woman on her husband, for that matter) is to be applauded, but there is a point at which such marital dedication can tip over into the realm of bad manners. Happily married couples must be aware that their devotion to each other can all too often look like the exclusion of everybody else. It is simply unkind, for example, to make a third party – who may very well be single – feel uncomfortable and embarrassed.

As two very lucky people, who are happy to be with each other, it is your responsibility to make people around you comfortable: this means taking the focus away from each other and turning your attention towards other people: no kissing; no pet names; no whispering; no giggling at private jokes. You will have plenty of time, and privacy, in which to enjoy each other's company – just try and ensure that other people enjoy being with you. *See also Affection, Public Displays of*

VALENTINE TO VULGARITY

VALENTINE

Although often tastelessly commercialised, the 14th of February provides an opportunity for the romantically inclined to celebrate love and relationships. It is wise to be relaxed about the whole thing, but take your cue from your beloved. Be particularly wary of those who noisily deride St. Valentine's Day, only to be disappointed or downright furious when they find themselves present-less and card-less come the big day. Some restaurants insist on offering themed menus, but unless your Valentine expects it, eateries are generally best avoided – the pressure can be stifling. If you are in the business of gift-giving, either spend serious cash on a dozen undeniably beautiful roses or opt for something more imaginative. A thoughtless offering is worse than nothing at all. For the unattached, anonymous cards have their own pitfalls: you run the risk of being seen as either too feeble to come forward in person or, worse, as a stalker. Unless you are an incurable romantic – and a patient one at that – there is no need to wait for Valentine's Day to break your cover.

VALET PARKING

Widely available in the USA, you will probably only encounter valet parking in more exclusive hotels and clubs in the UK, and at places – such as airports – that offer a (paid) valet parking service. If you unexpectedly encounter complementary valet parking, react with aplomb. Hand your keys to the attendant and walk away without a backward

glance; never apologise about the state of your car, or
plead with them to drive carefully. When they return the car,
and if you are satisfied with the service (i.e. you haven't been
made to wait too long and your precious vehicle is none
the worse for wear), then offer them a tip (minimum £1).
See also Hotels; Tipping

VEGETARIANS

Vegetarians, vegans, pescatarians, coeliacs, non-dairy,
macrobiotic — not to mention kosher and halal — it's a
wonder any of us still cook for each other when there are
so many dietary pitfalls along the way. With the huge increase
in allergies, intolerances and food dogmas, eating has
become fearsomely complicated.

Nowadays, the recipe for success when dealing with
vegetarians *et al* is a generous dose of tolerance topped up
with genuine culinary curiosity as to how you can cook for
them without producing something boring and stereotypical
— but spiced up with some resolve not to let their food
issues take over your entire gourmet preparation. Don't go
overboard to please a vegetarian at the expense of your more
numerous carnivore friends; it is enough to provide a little
something extra beyond the side vegetables you've prepared
for everyone else.

The basic etiquette surrounding vegetarianism (and
other food issues) and dining out with friends is that you
ring the hostess a couple of days beforehand, to warn her
about what you can or can't eat. But don't take this too far —

vegans, for example, should simply eat before they come out and content themselves with the side veg. Pity the poor hostess who was told, "I'm vegetarian but I'm also dairy intolerant, so no cheese. I can't bear vegetarian hippy food like nut roasts so none of that please. Oh, and I'm iron-deficient so could you build that in as well?" A gracious acknowledgement from a vegetarian that theirs is not the majority view encourages tolerance: being faddy does not.

VISITORS, UNEXPECTED

'Santa Claus has the right idea. Visit people once a year.'
VICTOR BORGE

It is obviously the height of good manners to be hospitable under all circumstances; it is clearly the height of bad manners to turn up unannounced and expect someone to be hospitable towards you when they've had no warning. So how do you treat the unexpected visitor? How much onus is on you, the reluctant but impeccably-mannered host? Friends who've popped in for a surprise cup of tea should be welcomed warmly if you have time for their visit; but it is entirely within the bounds of good manners to tell them straight if you're too busy to spend more than a few minutes with them.

Staying guests require equally firm handling because they have broken the unspoken rule that says you let someone know when you're coming to see them; they should be happy to get clean sheets, a roof over their head and matter-of-fact instructions as to what is available to eat in the fridge and store cupboards. Restrain the impulse to say, "If only I had known you were coming, I would have been able to entertain you properly," because this undoes all the good work of being hospitable in the first place. Having turned up unexpectedly, the visitor should then not compound their error by lingering. If you are suffering from a visitor who is outstaying the initial surprised welcome, try treating them like the rest of the family. If they don't leave then, they never will. Finally, if you are someone who has been lucky enough to be an unexpected visitor who was welcomed with open arms, don't make the mistake of repeating your gaffe. *See also Guests, House*

VOICEMAIL

Leave a personalised message on your phone so that people know they have got through to the correct person. Be meticulous about returning messages; don't use your voicemail as an indiscriminate way of fobbing off callers. If you are leaving a voicemail message don't ramble; be concise and leave your name and a contact number. *See also Mobile Phones*

VPL

In this age of seam-free knickers and thongs there's really no excuse for a VPL. Choose appropriate underwear for your outfit and check in the mirror (front and back) before leaving the house. *See also Underwear*

VULGARITY

'Vulgarity begins when the imagination succumbs to the explicit.'
DORIS DAY

Given that vulgarity is defined by the OED as first, 'the common people' and second, 'the quality of lacking taste and refinement', it is easy to become po-faced and snobbish when discussing it. Where vulgarity becomes relevant to modern manners is in the sense of being inappropriately showy or showing off. Often the line between extravagant and vulgar is perilously fine. A splendidly-imagined party frock can easily become an OTT, vulgar liability; a generous offer to pay for a group of friends' dinners can be interpreted as a vulgar flash of cash. Arthur Schopenhauer nailed it severely when he said, 'Will, minus intellect, constitutes vulgarity.'

In our modern age, extravagance and flamboyance are ever-more acceptable; but if you're not sure where the tipping point into vulgarity comes, then play safe and rein in a little just in case. Even if you do slide into vulgarity ever so slightly, don't be too fussed: censure only creeps in where there is concealment – where vulgarity is used to shield someone's true nature and becomes affectation; the 'Hyacinth Bouquet' syndrome. Above all, don't be snooty – condemning others for their vulgarity is, frankly, rather vulgar in and of itself.

WAGON, ON THE TO **WINE**

WAGON, ON THE

'Once, during Prohibition, I was forced to live for days on nothing but food and water.'
W.C. FIELDS

Most people, at some point in their life, refrain from alcohol. On occasions, refusal of alcohol is for perfectly clear medical reasons (booze may clash with prescription drugs, or an operation is impending, or the person is pregnant). At other times, it is more clearly a case of self-imposed abstinence: this can range from a few weeks 'clean-living' to a committed campaign to kick the drink habit once and for all.

Whatever the reason, a decision has been made, and must be respected. As a host, you may be confronted with a refusal of drink from your guest. Never question why this is happening; never cajole, or plead, or tease. You may be understandably disappointed that they're not joining in the party fun, but you must never let this show – meet their refusal with good grace, and offer a tempting range of alcohol-free drinks.

If you are the teetotaller (however temporary), you must also mind your manners. Refuse a drink politely; give an explanation if you think that helps. Never act the martyr, miserably cradling your mineral water as the party takes off around you. Never lecture your fellow guests about the benefits of an alcohol-free existence. If you are sober, intoxicated company can be baffling; conversations meander, arguments break out for no reason, non-jokes are met with general hilarity. If you are unable to cope with this alcohol-induced anarchy, don't go to the party. If you can endure these antics without a censorious air, you will be worth your weight in gold – the one sober guest at the end of the evening who is able to sort out the increasingly unruly guests, and even drive them safely home. *See also Drunkenness*

WASTEFUL, BEING

Modern society makes it almost impossible to avoid taking more than you need. Consumers have round-the-clock access to everything we never knew we wanted, but the pressure to cut down on wastefulness is growing. Knowingly squandering resources appears selfish and unneighbourly. It is worth spending a little time identifying your excesses and making a few simple changes to shopping habits, energy use and so on to ensure that your consumption is proportionate. A word to the zealous, however: though it is perfectly laudable to be principled on the subject, be careful not to become a waste-watching bore. *See also Eco-Etiquette*

WEATHER, TALKING ABOUT

'It is commonly observed, that when two Englishmen meet, their first talk is of the weather.'
SAMUEL JOHNSON

English people are notorious for their endless fascination with the weather, a topic that is deployed nationwide as an ice-breaker. When two strangers meet, in a train or a queue for example, it is virtually *de rigueur* to enjoy a short conversation about the weather. The primary function of this fascination with the weather is, of course, to break down the English person's natural reserve; it offers a universal, and neutral, topic, which everyone, from a small child to an elderly grandmother, enjoys discussing. Other countries endure far more noteworthy weather events – droughts, hurricanes, tornadoes – but the English weather is, above all, unpredictable. Sunshine, showers, wind and rain sweep across the country with extraordinary rapidity, providing an ever-changing outlook. And in these days of global warming, English people can now enjoy discussing ever more unpredictable weather – blizzards in April, floods in July, and so on. With the weather as a topic, conversation is never going to falter. *See also Conversation*

WEDDING LISTS

The circumstances and age of the bride and bridegroom often influence the choice of wedding list and presents. A young couple setting up home will have clear priorities, which will be very different to the expectations of an older, established couple who already live together.

Lists are available through department stores, specialist wedding list companies, independent shops or charities. Guests are able to buy in-store, online or over the phone. It is unusual to ask for money; some couples request contributions or gift vouchers towards the cost of their honeymoon. Most couples include details of the wedding list with the invitations.

Guests should not think that they are being unoriginal by buying from the list — the couple has specifically requested those items. However, a guest is free to do something different if they would like to give a unique or individual present. It is a gracious gesture for guests who are unable to attend to give a present. *See also Presents*

WEDDINGS, ATTENDING

Weddings are special occasions and guests should feel privileged that they have been invited. The wishes of the bride and groom should be respected — it is, after all, *their* day. There may be a policy on children or seemingly inconvenient timings, but guests must remember that the day is the culmination of months of planning, and should be flexible and fit in accordingly.

Accommodation, if required, should be booked well in advance; the host will usually recommend somewhere local or have secured a block-booking. Remember to check whether there is any transport laid on, or if you need to book a taxi.

Presents are either bought in advance from the couple's list, or you may prefer to take something along on the day. There is usually an area at the reception for guests to deposit presents — make sure your gift is clearly labelled.

Guests should be appropriately dressed. Dress codes are not included on a wedding invitation unless guests are required to adhere to an uncustomary code (such as black tie). It is, however, traditional for men to wear morning dress, or a suit with a shirt and tie. Women should look elegant in a suit or dress – appropriate for the season and the weather – and may also wear a hat. Head-to-toe outfits in white or cream should never be worn and all black, unless cleverly accessorised, may look troublingly sombre.

Wedding guests should familiarise themselves with the order of the day. Be punctual for the ceremony and help the ushers by telling them if you are a guest of the bride or groom (or both), friend or family. Be warned: weddings are usually a long day, with unusual meal times and many celebratory drinks and toasts. Guests should pace themselves to ensure that they last the course. *See also Hats*

WEIGHT, DISCUSSING

'When we lose twenty pounds... we may be losing the twenty best pounds we have! We may be losing the pounds that contain our genius, our humanity, our love and honesty.'
WOODY ALLEN

It seems to be a contemporary truism that a low weight is desirable. This is not the place to discuss the health and psychological implications of assuming that the lower the weight, the better, but even so it is surely plain bad manners to single out the people who are not close enough to that mythical low weight. Nearly all of us are not the weight we would ideally like to be (or the weight that society would like us to be). Discussing weight takes up more airtime, in more gym changing rooms, round more office water coolers and in more coffee shops than any other subject except, perhaps, the weather. From the 'does my bum look big in this?' anthemic chant to a debate over one of the dozen or so diet titles published each month, there is no longer anything sacred or private about the subject of one's shape. Vital statistics are now vital stays of conversation.

In our narcissistic age, the code of conduct is as follows: any discussion of your own weight is, while tedious, acceptable unless you are being boastful. Any discussion of other's weights is still beyond the pale. Above all, never feel so liberated by your ability to discuss your own weight that you think this gives you some sort of *carte blanche* to introduce someone else to the party; comments along the lines of, "I've been doing this fabulous diet, perhaps you should try it?" are never going to be welcomed, no matter how flabby the focus of your question is. It's equally unfair when a woman asks a man if she is fat; this is an invitation for him to commit *hara-kiri* there and then — and remember that, in sexual politics, being self-assured and shapely is far more appealing than being scrawny and screwy. Never, ever discuss a woman's weight in the context of her being pregnant — if you make a false assumption about weight and pregnancy, you will never, ever be forgiven ... *See also Diets; Hunger; Zero*

WELLINGTON BOOTS

Wellies have, in recent years, become a fashion accessory. They are, however, made for mud and puddles, not pavements. So, use them for their correct, practical purpose, whether in Gloucestershire fields or at

Glastonbury Festival. Thick socks are a must. Muddy
boots should always be discarded at the door; those who
thoroughly clean their boots will quickly reveal themselves
as a countryside amateur.

WHINING

'It takes a genius to whine appealingly.'
F. SCOTT FITZGERALD

Whining is an abomination. It also Does Not Work. Even
if, by sheer persistence, your whining beats your target down
until they agree to everything, it's a pyrrhic victory. They
have either lost the will to live (in which case your reward
is literally short-lived) or they resent and despise you for
forcing them into doing something that they had initially
not contemplated doing. Meanwhile, everyone in the
vicinity resents and despises you and them for all the
whining in the first place. To some people – usually parents
of small children – whining becomes like wallpaper; it's
always there in the background but they no longer notice
it. But others surely do – and to them it is the height of
offensive noise pollution.

Nowadays we also have institutional whining – that
ranting, defensive note so common to the letters pages,
blog sites and any bus stop. Even unhappy lovers are no
longer star-crossed and blessed with Shakespearean ways
of expressing their unhappiness – nowadays, the hurdles
of love are more often raised by whinging about the
inadequacies (physical, mental, emotional) of their

partner, all expressed in the whiney lingo of barely-understood psychobabble. The lessons are clear: don't ever give whining clearance for take-off. Give in once to whining and you have given it wings to carry on flying ad infinitum. Don't whine yourself, no matter what the provocation — you're better than that.

WHISKY/WHISKEY

The obvious question of the spelling should rarely concern you when it comes to selecting a whisk(e)y; the chances are that your beverage will identify itself far more precisely than by its country of origin. But, for the record, whiskey with an 'e' is produced in Ireland or in the USA, while everywhere else forgoes the extra letter. A blended whisky is composed of a blend of single grain and single malt whiskies that have been distilled at more than one distillery. There are a number of commercial brands available and you can be pretty sure that the taste will be consistent. Single malts are produced from malted barley at a single distillery. They vary considerably in character and appreciating them can become a life's work. Bourbon is made in the USA, primarily from corn, and is distilled in oak casks.

Whisky should be drunk however you like it best; adding water or ice to a single malt is no longer frowned upon by the *cognoscenti*. Diluting blended whisky with soft drinks, such as lemonade or ginger ale, is also acceptable. Whisky is best imbibed from a heavy-based crystal glass to concentrate the aroma.

WHISPERING

'Alas! they had been friends in youth; but whispering tongues can poison truth.'

SAMUEL TAYLOR COLERIDGE

Whispering is a crude weapon of social rejection; by advertising intimacy with the person whose ear you're tickling, you are also patently excluding everyone else. It inevitably induces paranoia in the people around you, and at the very least makes them feel uncomfortable. In a group situation, you should never whisper something to one person that you don't feel comfortable conveying to the whole group. If you want to share a secret, save it for later.

Whispering to your companion when you're at the cinema, theatre or a concert, is deeply inconsiderate of the people around you. No matter how quietly you think you're talking, your whispering will be audible, and maddeningly distracting. Wait for a more appropriate setting. *See also Gossip; Secrets*

WHISTLING

If you're prone to whistling, be aware that you may be doing it unconsciously. People will be very irritated if they are forced to listen to your musical renditions in quiet areas — trains, museums, offices and so on. Essentially, whistling is done for the whistler's enjoyment, and as such, indulging in private is the safest course of action. Whistling to capture attention, especially through your fingers, is only appropriate on the sports pitch or the playground.

WHITE TIE

'With an evening coat ... anyone, even a stockbroker, can gain a reputation for being civilised.'
OSCAR WILDE

White tie — also referred to as 'full evening dress' — is the most formal, and rare, of dress codes, worn in the evening for royal ceremonies and balls. It may also be specified for formal evening weddings. Traditional white tie consists of:

- Black single-breasted tail coat with silk lapels, worn unbuttoned (never to be confused with a morning coat).
- Black trousers to match the tail coat, with two lines of braid down each outside leg.
- White marcella shirt, worn with a detachable wing collar, cufflinks and studs.
- Thin, white, hand-tied marcella bow-tie.
- White marcella evening waistcoat — double or single-breasted.
- Black patent lace-up shoes and black silk socks.

    In winter, a black overcoat and white silk scarf can be worn. Nowadays, it is rare to wear a top hat and many see it as a pointless exercise as it is only worn *en route* to the event, and therefore generally goes unnoticed. *See also Black Tie*

WIGS

No matter how eccentric the toupee or synthetic the wig, you must never snigger, point or pass comment. There are many reasons for wearing a wig — some go well beyond vanity or self-delusion — so don't let your mirth get the better of you.

WILES, FEMININE

Women have a whole panoply of techniques to help them
get what they want. They can enhance their sexual allure
with make-up, high heels and low-cut tops; they can flirt
outrageously; when all else fails, they can burst into tears.
Deploying these wiles in a working environment is, however,
fraught with difficulties. Certainly, when a woman's head
is butting against the glass ceiling, it may seem expedient to
use every trick in the book. And many women would argue
that they are merely reacting, in a uniquely femine way, to
the exclusion that can be generated by male bonding: after-
office drinking, sports clubs, rounds of golf and so on. Just
be aware that too vigorous an application of the feminine
arts may well mean that your career advancement is regarded
with cynical disapproval by male and female colleagues alike.
See also Feminism

WIND

Blame the dog, even if there isn't one. *See also Bodily Functions*

WINE

'Let us have wine and women, mirth and laughter,
Sermons and soda-water the day after.'
LORD BYRON

The original social lubricant, wine is a remarkable substance
with a unique ability to fascinate and delight, perplex and
terrify. This is partly because the world of wine boasts

infinite variety. But it's also because wine is a social drink that appears shrouded in mystery to the uninitiated. Happily, there are few serious gaffes that you can commit when confronted with a wine list. Many restaurants helpfully provide descriptions and suggested food pairings, and if a restaurant is clued-up enough to offer an extensive list, the chances are that there will be someone on hand to advise you on an appropriate choice. Asking for advice is always better than pretending you know more than you do, and it shows that you are interested rather than opting for the same safe bet every time. Ditto taking your time and waiting until you know what people will be eating before ordering a complementary wine. Somebody has to take control of ordering, but that person should not necessarily select the wine single-handed. Aim to satisfy all palates and take the time to establish what people are planning to eat. Ordering by the glass can solve the problem of seriously diverging tastes or irreconcilable dinner choices, but it's less convivial and certainly more expensive.

More often than not, it's possible to find a wine to please everyone. If you ordered, you will usually be asked to taste it. The waiter will show you the bottle and the cork so that you can verify your wine's identity. The nominated taster will then be served a very small amount in his or her glass. This is not your opportunity to decide whether you like the wine; you're simply checking that it's fit to drink. If it's not, you will know immediately. It should smell clean – the merest hint of sherry or a musty aroma indicates a problem. If everything seems in order, take a small sip. There is absolutely no need for ostentatious sniffing, swirling and gargling. Once you have nodded, everyone else will be served. There is no shame in buying a screw-cap bottle of wine. The humble twisty cap eliminates the risk of corking, and many well-regarded wine manufacturers are now turning to the screw cap, particularly for wines that are intended for early drinking.

Restaurants vary in their approach to topping up glasses. It is usual for the waiter to keep an eye on supplies, but if they don't, ensure that nobody's glass is ever empty. Dealing with wine outside a restaurant is usually less fraught. It is fine to take wine along to a dinner party as a gift, but don't expect it to be opened on the night. Presumably your host will have planned which wines to serve with dinner. Always keep a decent bottle in the fridge at home — impromptu celebrations demand it. Don't be intimidated by those self-proclaimed experts who demand to know which flavours you can detect. Smile, pronounce it delicious and avoid the question — at least you haven't fallen into the trap of making a boring exhibition of your ignorance.

X-RATED TO **ZZZZZ**

X-RATED

'Anything goes' is, for some, the root of all our woes; where tolerance tips over into negligence and X-rated becomes a recommendation not a prohibition. For others, the rules and regulations behind the X-rate are seen as yet another example of the baleful influence of the nanny state on our freedom. Rules are hemming in our natural impulses — the sex, violence and bad language that decide the X-rated label are a fact of life, they argue, so what right has some anonymous ratings board got to decide what we should or shouldn't listen to, watch or say?

It is all about consideration, plain and simple. Even the hardiest of antisocials don't actively teach their children to live by the laws of sex, violence and bad language; they might just fail to set them a good example to follow. So if X-rated behaviour in real life is generally condemned, then why fail to follow that up in the media? It's merely a case of joining up the dots — and realising that the watersheds, parental blocks on computers and cinema certificates are just the media's version of the closed doors and privacy of real life. It's just that we decide the latter and someone else decides the former based on the premise that we don't live in a world peopled purely by consenting, mature adults but one that contains innocent children, sensitive religious types and people of different moral values.

There is undoubtedly something in the mature human condition that gets a kick out of sex, violence and even bad language — is this not all the more reason to keep it rarefied and not become inured to it as an everyday occurrence?

XENOPHOBIA

Most of us, when confronted by a rant about foreigners-coming-over-here-and-taking-our-jobs, have probably taken the most pusillanimous route – the weak murmuring that could either be assent or terribly polite, non-confrontational disagreement – and most of us would probably feel a little shamed and tainted as a result. If you fall into this camp – not xenophobic, generally embracing the dissolving of national barriers because it means that race, nationalism and religion cease to be such dividers and your Polish plumber is just excellent – then your path is tricky but your steps are ultimately towards a moral high ground. If you are truly xenophobic, and resent and loathe the foreign influences that are permeating your country, be aware that slurring people just because they are foreign hits the 'generalisations are rude' button and no amount of 'I don't hate foreigners but I hate the way they've ... ' cop-outs are going to get you off the hook.

If you are faced with xenophobia and are unsure how to react without endangering your own safety, there are two options. One is to show the sort of intense interest that a TV naturalist shows in the nocturnal activities of a badger, bombarding the ranter with detailed questions until you've skewered the xenophobe on his own point. Another tack, which could get you bogged down in discussion, is to attack the obvious hypocrisy of modern xenophobia – point out that, over the last 200 years, our culture has been unarguably enriched by Empire, other cultures, other nations. *See also Racism*

XL

'I have more flesh than another man, and therefore more frailty.'
WILLIAM SHAKESPEARE

The obesity epidemic fills our newspapers, airwaves and world wide web. It is indeed a fact of life that there are more hugely fat people in our society than ever before. So how should we react to the extra large? And how should the extra large be expected to behave? We all know that we should not sit in judgement – that even if a fat person is fat because they like cakes (rather than because they have a metabolic or glandular problem) that should not affect the way we judge them, relate to them or rate them. But tell that to the children in an academic study who identified fat children as the first people they would avoid in a playground, even 'hate'. Much as we would like to change the world into a place where size, colour and all other external qualifiers simply do not matter, 'isms' will never die.

What we can do is preach a 'live and let live' tolerance. Being scornful of that XL person who lumbers, breathless, up to the bus stop, who then has to wait until there are two adjacent seats free because they can't fit in one, is just the final straw in a daily catalogue of embarrassments and humiliations; so why not be kind instead? But tolerance works two ways. If you are obese yourself, be tolerant both of yourself and of others – every fat person has glared at a thin person and dared them to say or do something horrible; how much happier you would be if you stepped out confident that there is nothing 'wrong' with you and that thin people aren't necessarily the enemy?

XMAS

Although it is said that the word Xmas traces back over many centuries, as a general rule, Christmas should be called Christmas, not Xmas.

YAWNING

'Life is too short, and the time we waste in yawning never can be regained.'
STENDHAL

Try, whenever possible, to refrain from yawning; if you must do so, cover your mouth with your hand and mutter an apology. Don't inflict your fatigue on other people — if you're too tired to socialise without a gaping mouth and watering eyes, you should be tucked up in your bed. It is even more offensive to yawn out of boredom; if you're reduced to a state of jaw-aching tedium, make your excuses and go before your behaviour causes real offence.

YOGA

Practising yoga requires calm; don't burst late into the class huffing and puffing. Slip in silently at the back or, if over ten minutes late, give it up. Turn off your mobile. Don't chat during the class and don't groan or protest with each new position. If the poses really are too hard, try your best to get as near as possible to what is expected. Respect the aura at all times. Don't wear old, holey kit — the stretches will either exacerbate the problem or reveal more than you'd like.

ZEBRA CROSSINGS

A zone of voluntary courtesy in our increasingly prescriptive road system, zebra crossings should be treated with respect. Drivers should slow down when approaching one, and check for waiting pedestrians, or people who are approaching the crossing. Wait until they have crossed the road before you move away; never rev your engine as people are crossing the road. If you can't treat zebra crossings with patience and courtesy, think of the alternative – yet another set of traffic lights. *See also Driving; Road Rage*

ZERO

For some, the term 'zero' has become a description of the ultimate loser – not a hero but a zero. For others, 'zero' has become a shining beacon of ambition, a Holy Grail of self-control and self-fulfilment. No matter that size zero is actually an American term and that here it's a slightly less dramatic sounding size four – we all know that being size zero is the ultimate goal of anyone who wants to be the last word in thin. It's not hard to see why – the women in our magazines are almost airbrushed away, our Hollywood celebrities would rather resemble a lollipop than be fleshier than their peers and the craze for surgical desizing is getting out of hand.

The trouble is that common sense seems to have been sucked out of such people along with all that liposuctioned fat. The trashier end of the media is loud in its condemnation when a hitherto Size Zero 'piles on the pounds', drowning out the health warnings from nutritionists and doctors, and ignoring the heartfelt cries from men who say that they like their women with some flesh to grab on to.

It's obviously rude to criticise someone for wanting to be a size zero, no matter how deranged you might think they are. It is equally ill-mannered to sneer at someone who is already a size zero – they might be naturally emaciated and longing to put some weight on, or they may have finally achieved their own ambition to achieve ultra-skinniness; who are you to point out the likelihood of osteoporosis and infertility? If you yourself are a size zero or would like to be a size zero, don't be arrogant and assume that anyone who genuinely doesn't care about what size they are is somehow defective. The slim shall not inherit the earth, just the occasional discounted designer sample. Anyone who believes that their 'perfect' vital statistics make them 'perfect' in other ways is no hero but a true zero. *See also Diets; Weight, Discussing*

ZIPS

If you spot someone emerging from the lavatory with their zip down, weigh up the situation and embark on the path of minimal embarrassment. If their shirt (or worse) is on display, the chances are that others will notice. Whatever your approach, discretion is critical. If you are on friendly terms, by all means take them to one side and indicate their omission, but never smile first. It is a rare being who doesn't blush when they realise, so handle it delicately. If you are

hoping that they will become a business associate, it may
be wise to keep your lips sealed and your eyes firmly above
belt level. However, there are no hard and fast rules, and
you should rely on your judgement. If someone draws your
attention to your own zip, trust that they have your best
interests at heart, smile confidentially and thank them
for saving you any further discomfiture.

ZZZZZ

Make sure you get sufficient sleep. If you're over-tired,
you'll become irritable, short-tempered and liable to
mis-judge situations. Dropping off in public is only
ever acceptable on aeroplanes. *See also Awake, Staying*